Harry Potter
WIZARDS UNITE

D1165978

By Stephen Stratton

Scholastic Inc.

WIZARDING
WORLD

NIANTIC

WB
GAMES™

PORTKEY
GAMES™

Library of Congress Cataloging-in-Publication Data available

ISBN 978-1-338-25396-2

10 9 8 7 6 5 4 3 2 1   19 20 21 22 23

Printed in the U.S.A.   40

First printing 2019

Book design by Cheung Tai

TABLE OF CONTENTS

INTRODUCTION

"We are only as strong as we are united, as weak as we are divided."

—*Albus Dumbledore*

Welcome to *Harry Potter: Wizards Unite*. If you're reading this guidebook, you've downloaded the game and are ready to answer the Ministry of Magic's call to join the Statute of Secrecy Task Force. This guide should prove to be a fun and informative resource on your many journeys through the wonders of the game.

HOW TO USE THIS BOOK

Chapter One: Magic Is All Around You (p. 8)

You never know what sorts of magical happenings might pop up as you explore the world in *Harry Potter: Wizards Unite*. This chapter offers you the scoop on each one to help you master the basics! Flip ahead a few pages to learn all about every place, object, and encounter that might appear on the **MAP** as you explore.

Chapter Two: Realize Your Wizard Potential! (p. 42)

After you've learned how to navigate the map and the many things to do, it's important to develop your skills as a **WIZARD**. This chapter focuses on the intricacies of wizardry advancement, including overviews of each **WIZARDING STAT** and **PROFESSION**, complete with insights into each Profession's Lesson Plan. The chapter rounds out with a detailed analysis of the fine art of **POTION** brewing—a skill you'll need to advance faster through the game.

Chapter Three: Extraordinary Events (p. 72)

Adventure waits around every corner in the wizarding world, but during certain times of the month or year, special **EVENTS** are happening. Here you'll learn more about the events that occur throughout the year, along with **DAILY TASKS** and those unusual **ODDITIES**.

Chapter Four: Wizards Unite! (p. 78)

Exploring the world can be fun on your own, but flying solo isn't quite as easy when you're faced with fearsome **FOES** in a **WIZARDING CHALLENGE**. If you're itching to fight through a **FORTRESS**, turn to this chapter to learn how to handle yourself after your Runestones have been set.

Chapter Five: Calamity Case File (p. 102)

As you hone your magic and return more and more **FOUNDABLES**, the mystery surrounding the **CALAMITY** grows more and more . . . *mysterious*. Who could have unleashed such a hazardous spell, and what can be done to stop it? Little by little, you'll discover Mystery Collectibles— clues that provide precious bits of insight into recent events, which are compiled in the **CALAMITY CASE FILE**. This exploratory chapter studies all the evidence and theories surrounding the Calamity up to this point.

Chapter Six: Lost and Foundables (p. 138)

The guide winds down with a complete inventory of the **PAGES** seen in the **EXPLORATION** and **CHALLENGE REGISTRIES**. Marvel at this array of completed Registry Pages, and get some tips to help you collect the **FRAGMENTS** you'll need to complete some of the rarer images!

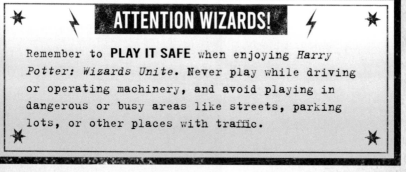

ATTENTION WIZARDS!

Remember to **PLAY IT SAFE** when enjoying *Harry Potter: Wizards Unite*. Never play while driving or operating machinery, and avoid playing in dangerous or busy areas like streets, parking lots, or other places with traffic.

✳ A CONFOUNDING CALAMITY ✳

The **WIZARDING WORLD** is in peril! Without warning, a disastrous **CALAMITY** has suddenly occurred. Everything that anyone has ever feared, revered, or held dear in the wizarding world—people, creatures, precious artifacts, even memories—has been stolen and displaced, tossed all across the world. You've got to return what is lost, and quickly, for the **STATUTE OF SECRECY** is under threat.

INTERNATIONAL STATUTE OF SECRECY

In 1692, after the persecution of wizards and witches by non-magical beings in Europe and North America, the International Confederation of Wizards passed the International Statute of Wizarding Secrecy. It requires wizards and witches to conceal their use of magic and keep the wizarding world secret from non-magical beings in order to protect magic-kind.

Playing as a gifted **WITCH** or **WIZARD**, you have been selected to help contain this terrible Calamity. You'll work closely with **CONSTANCE PICKERING**, a capable **MINISTRY** operative who holds a position alongside Hermione Granger on the **STATUTE OF SECRECY TASK FORCE**. In your role as a recent inductee to the S.O.S. Task Force, you'll have access to a special **REGISTRY OF FOUNDABLES** that tracks your progress as you venture to combat this alarming Calamity. Are you up for the challenge, wizard?

Good!

Then let's get started . . .

MINISTRY OF MAGIC

The Ministry of Magic, the center of wizarding government in the United Kingdom, is located deep underground in Whitehall, London. The Ministry upholds and enforces wizarding laws in the United Kingdom, and is divided into many different departments, including the Department of Magical Law Enforcement and the Department of Mysteries. The Ministry is leading the S.O.S. Task Force since the Calamity appears to have originated within the United Kingdom.

CHAPTER ONE

MAGIC IS ALL AROUND YOU

"Let us step into the night and pursue that flighty temptress, adventure."

—Albus Dumbledore

A s Dumbledore said in *Harry Potter and the Half-Blood Prince*, "Magic always leaves traces." *In Harry Potter: Wizards Unite*, these *Traces* can be found all around you—a whole world of magical mischief has been unleashed into everyday Muggle life. Playing as a gifted **WITCH** or **WIZARD**, you can see, hear, and interact with all sorts of incredible artifacts and fantastic beasts as you explore.

EXPLORING THE WIZARDING WORLD

You'll soon find there's no shortage of magical intrigue to take part in. The wizarding world is in peril, after all, with a host of magical beings and enchanted artifacts having been suddenly let loose on all of humanity—magic and Muggle alike. Only by working together with other valiant witches and wizards will you be able to set things right and save the wizarding world from disastrous exposure.

✳ THE MAP ✳

When you're exploring the world, you'll want to keep an eye on the **MAP**. Your Map reveals all manner of interesting items and magical locations. Simply tap on any object that appears on the Map to interact with it. Your position on the Map is tracked using the **MAGICAL ME** figure, which walks around the Map as you travel. While it's vital to remain aware of your surroundings while playing *Wizards Unite*, if you're a passenger in a car or train while playing, your Magical Me will fly on a broomstick!

Many of the Map's features are tied to real-world locations, including prominent landmarks such as statues, parks, and sporting venues. Read on to discover every-thing the Map might show you.

✳ ITEMS ✳

Whether brewing a Potion, activating a Portkey, or preparing for battle, a well-prepared wizard or witch always has plenty of useful **ITEMS** on hand. How does one find items in the first place? By exploring, of course!

As you journey across the land, glance at the Map to spot magical items that can pop up at any moment. The most common items by far are **POTION INGREDIENTS** (p. 65), but you may also come across valuable **PORTKEY PORTMANTEAUS** that can help you take magical journeys to secret areas of the wizarding world.

Some items require special conditions to appear on the Map. For example, certain items will only appear at specific times of day, under certain weather conditions, or during **PARTICULAR PHASES** of the moon. See p. 72 for details!

When any sort of item appears on the Map, simply tap it to stuff it into your **SUITCASE** for later use. As long as it appears on your Map, you will be able to collect it; no need to approach it directly.

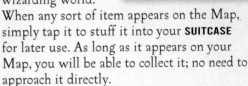

SUITCASE

Your Suitcase magically holds all your items, letting you carry loads of useful gadgets and gear on your journey. Simply tap the **SUITCASE ICON** to open your Suitcase and view its contents. While your Suitcase is equipped with a handy Undetectable Extension Charm, every charm has its limits. You will need to use **GOLD** to expand the charm—and your storage space—if you exceed its capacity.

✳ DIAGON ALLEY ✳

If you're in a pinch for items and have no time to wait, consider a quick trip to **DIAGON ALLEY**, where wizarding supplies are sold. Open your Suitcase and tap the **BASKET ICON** in the top right corner to. Swing by **GRINGOTTS** to trade real-world money for in-game **GOLD**, then buy some worthy wares at **WISEACRES**, where you can find Spell Energy, Dark Detectors, and Silver Keys. Or perhaps you'd prefer to pick up a few Potions at **SLUG & JIGGERS**, which can save you time and Potion Ingredients. You can visit Diagon Alley practically anytime, so keep it in mind.

WIZARDING GOLD

While exchanging your Muggle money at Gringotts is great in a pinch, there are other ways to acquire Gold in *Harry Potter: Wizards Unite*. Gold can be earned by completing all your Daily Tasks, successfully completing Trace Encounters, and leveling up.

✶ INNS ✶

As you progress through the game, you'll come across several different building icons on your map. These locations, called **INNS** are among the most common locations you'll see on the Map. Although they come in several assortments, all Inns function exactly alike. Simply approach and tap a nearby Inn to step inside.

Once inside an Inn, you'll find yourself seated by the window, which features a view of the real-world landmark outside. The chef wastes no time in whipping up a selection of delicious treats for you to devour—simply swipe the screen to see what's cooking!

Voilà! After you swipe, a delectable dish becomes yours. The **FOOD** that you receive at Inns restores varying amounts of **SPELL ENERGY**, which is required to cast spells in **COMBAT** or **TRACE ENCOUNTERS**. While something light like a cauldron of soup or pumpkin juice only restores one or two units of Spell Energy, larger meals and heartier drinks like Butterbeer can restore seven units of Spell Energy or more.

PYRAMID FOUNTAINS

31/75

RETURN IN 4:12 TO COLLECT
MORE SPELL ENERGY.

INN   X   DARK DETECTORS

While it would be nice to swipe again to regain your full Spell Energy more quickly, you'll need to wait while the chef cooks the next course. A five-minute timer pops up after you've received your treat, indicating the delay before you can swipe again. If you're in a rush for more Spell Energy head to another Inn nearby.

You will notice a slight change to an Inn's appearance on the Map after you've eaten: Smoke is now piping from the Inn's chimney. This subtle effect tells you that the next meal isn't quite ready yet. Return when the smoke is gone to harvest more Spell Energy.

All wizards and witches can obtain Food from a single Inn, so there's no need to wait if a friend has recently enjoyed a snack there.

As if providing restorative Food weren't enough, Inns also serve another equally valuable purpose: Every Inn features a wild-looking device known as an **AMPLIFIER** that's stashed in the back room. Once powered by a **DARK DETECTOR**, the Amplifier automatically boosts **TRACES** of magic in the Inn's vicinity, causing rarer and higher-threat Traces to appear on the Map near the Inn for a brief time! Tap the Dark Detectors button at the bottom of your screen to discover the Amplifier, then tap the Place button to place a Dark Detector. The number of Dark Detectors in your Suitcase can be seen in the top left corner of your screen.

DARK DETECTOR

Dark Detectors are magical devices that can be used to detect hidden things or someone with ill intent is hanging about. Famed Auror Alastor Moody frequently employed Dark Detectors, and Harry Potter owned a Dark Detector or two (Sneakoscopes) during his time at Hogwarts.

As you might suspect, Dark Detectors are quite valuable. You'll occasionally receive them as rewards from the Ministry for leveling up, and you can also purchase them in Diagon Alley. Once found, they're stored in your **VAULT**, ready for use at your convenience.

Up to three Dark Detectors can be set on a single Amplifier, providing ever-increasing benefits. Filling the Amplifier with all three Dark Detectors provides a tremendous boost to nearby Traces, greatly improving the odds that rare Traces will appear nearby. Best of all, every wizard and witch near the Inn can benefit from an Amplifier's effects, so a Dark Detector placed by your friend provides its benefits to you, and vice versa. Multiple wizards can place their Dark Detectors on the same Amplifier as well, working together to maximize amplification.

It's easy to see if an Inn's Amplifier has been activated: Back on the Map screen, a swirl of magic will be encircling the Inn. This little swirl tells you the Amplifier is working, and you're sure to notice several Traces popping up nearby. The more Dark Detectors that are used, the more magic you'll see! Remember, you can benefit from Dark Detectors placed by other wizards and witches as well, so seek out Inns that feature these swirls to find super-rare Traces nearby!

✳ GREENHOUSES ✳

Less common than Inns, **GREENHOUSES** are similarly cozy locations that contain magical flora, which wizards and witches can harvest to obtain valuable **INGREDIENTS** for brewing **POTIONS**. Some Ingredients are quite rare, and certain Ingredients are much easier to obtain by visiting Greenhouses. Turn to p. 65 for details.

Tap a nearby Greenhouse to enter it and view the vegetation within. Pick a pot and swipe up to collect your Ingredients, which are swiftly stashed in your **VAULT**. If you're lucky, you might even score some other sorts of items! But Ingredients are the main treat you'll find at Greenhouses.

Back in
4M 50S

Like the restorative Food you get from Inns, it takes a while for a Greenhouse's plant life to grow after it's been harvested. A familiar timer appears, letting you know that it'll be five minutes before more Ingredients can be gathered. Head out to find another Greenhouse if you're in urgent need of Ingredients, or simply wait for more to sprout at your current location. Because Greenhouses are somewhat uncommon, it can be useful to find a few in proximity to one another and travel between them.

Also, like Inns, a Greenhouse's outside appearance changes after you've harvested its Ingredients: A red flag is hoisted high. This helps you track the Greenhouses you've recently visited. When the flag is taken down, you're free to forage once more.

MINISTRY OF MAGIC

The Ministry has ensured that Greenhouses contain unique Ingredients for all wizards and witches. Should your friend harvest a Greenhouse's goods before you, you're still free to step inside and gather some Ingredients for yourself—no waiting required!

★ FORTRESSES ★

Ranking among the rarest Map locations, **FORTRESSES** are towering, imposing structures that house some of the most thrilling and perilous combat-based encounters: **WIZARDING CHALLENGES**. While these aren't the only places to find them, you can look for Fortresses in places where people tend to gather, such as parks, scenic lookouts, and other landmarks in your area. These sites serve as fantastic spots to team up with other players to tackle the many trials that await within the Fortress's walls.

All Fortresses function in much the same way: Each Fortress plays host to a number of Wizarding Challenges, which pit you and your allies against hordes of beasts, shady spellcasters, and other dangerous **FOES**.

While it's possible to tackle Fortresses on your own, it's also quite dangerous; you're much better off finding a few fellow wizards to fight alongside. Don't be shy; ask a friend (or four) to join you in your quest to complete each Fortress's Wizarding Challenges.

MAGICAL GAMES AND SPORTS TREASURE TRUNK

You're free to visit Fortresses any time you like, but Wizarding Challenges can only be started using special items known as **RUNESTONES**. Unearth these rare rocks by seeking out **TRACES** of magic and returning the **FOUNDABLES** you discover, thereby filling in your **REGISTRY PAGES**. As you level up each section of your Registry, you'll regularly receive **TREASURE TRUNKS** that are likely to land you some Runestones. See p. 22 for more on Traces, and p. 28 to learn all about the Registry.

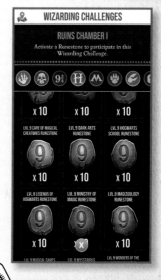

Once you've found a Runestone, you're ready to attempt a Fortress's Wizarding Challenges. Head inside to visit the **ROOM OF RUNESTONES**, where you're required to place a Runestone to advance. The level of Runestone you choose impacts the level of difficulty for the upcoming Challenge along with the quality of your rewards, so choose wisely! Each wizard must use a Runestone in order to advance to the trial, where **COMBAT** awaits!

Up to five wizards can attempt a Wizarding Challenge at once. If you don't have a friend nearby, you can still play in a group. You will automatically be queued with a group of nearby wizards if any are available and entering the same Wizarding Challenge in the Fortress at the same time as you.

Yearning to learn more about Fortresses, Combat, and Wizarding Challenges? Flip to p. 78 to find a whole chapter filled with all the info you need!

LANDMARK FLAGS are among the most important location points you'll see on the Map. These special flags indicate that TRACES of a particular FAMILY of magic are likely to be found nearby, helping you track down the specific Traces you need to complete each PAGE in the REGISTRY. More about Traces can be found on p. 22.

MORE MAGICAL GAMES AND SPORTS TRACES CAN BE FOUND HERE.

FAMILY ICONS

The FAMILY ICON on a Landmark Flag's banner signifies the Family of magic to which it belongs, and this Icon directly relates to the Registry. Tap the Landmark for more info, and notice that a region of the MAP briefly lights up. This highlighted area is the place to search when you're in need of specific Traces.

Once you've located a Landmark Flag, take your time exploring the highlighted zone. While Traces of any Family of magic might still appear, you're more likely to find the sorts of Traces that match the flag. Visit the local Inns and use Dark Detectors to activate their Amplifiers, thereby increasing your odds of finding even more Traces!

Landmarks are a big help when it comes to completing specific Registry Pages, but first, you need to find those Flags. The following chart can help you track down Landmark Flags for nine of the ten Families (turn to page 34 for more information about the tenth family, "Oddities"). Use it to help you locate Landmark Flags, then begin your search for Traces of the **FOUNDABLES** that you seek.

CARE OF MAGICAL CREATURES
Parks

DARK ARTS
Banks

HOGWARTS SCHOOL
Colleges and Libraries

LEGENDS OF HOGWARTS
Historical Locations

MINISTRY OF MAGIC
Government Buildings

MAGIZOOLOGY
Zoo and Animal Locations

MAGICAL GAMES AND SPORTS
Sports Locations

MYSTERIOUS ARTIFACTS
Shops and Stores

WONDERS OF THE WIZARDING WORLD
Arts and Entertainment Locations

✳ TRACES OF MAGIC ✳

Visiting all these Map locations is sure to keep you busy, but *Wizards Unite* hasn't just tasked you with sightseeing. Your main mission as a member of the **STATUTE OF SECRECY TASK FORCE** is to seek out and return the magical **FOUNDABLES** that have somehow been scattered throughout the land. The Ministry will richly reward you each time you return a Foundable.

Your search for Foundables begins with tracking down the aforementioned **TRACES** of magic. As you explore the world, look for shimmering **TRACE ICONS** that materialize on the Map. When you see one, approach and tap it to examine the Foundable you've discovered.

Just like the Landmark Flags indicate, Traces come in ten different assortments, each one representing a different **Family**. It's handy to know each **Family Icon,** as they all relate to the **Registry**. What's more, certain Traces will only appear under special conditions, which may be related to the time of day or phase of the moon.

Also, be on the lookout for special Traces that feature red beams of light, for these hint at the presence of an extremely rare and dangerous Foundable. Traces that sport purple beams of light are **Brilliant Traces**—these are tied to special **Events** that occur throughout the year (see page 76).

Investigating a Trace shifts your screen from the Map to a **TRACE ENCOUNTER**, where you discover the Foundable that has created the Trace. Retrieving a Foundable isn't easy; each Foundable is guarded by a **CONFOUNDABLE**—a dangerous Calamity spell that has seemingly been cast as a last resort to keep the Foundables from running amok. You'll need to cast a specific spell to banish the Confoundable, return the Foundable to its proper place in the wizarding world, and end the threat of exposure. Naturally, the requisite spell varies depending on the Confoundable in question.

Foundables and Confoundables come in all shapes and sizes, and some can be quite difficult to deal with. A **THREAT LEVEL** appears at the start of each Encounter, indicating how great of a risk to the wizarding world the Foundable is, and how challenging the act of banishing the Confoundable is likely to be. The greater your skill as a wizard, the more likely you'll be to succeed!

If you're low on **SPELL ENERGY**, or if the Threat Level seems too high, you can end the Encounter yourself by tapping the **LEAVE** button at the top left of the screen. The Trace will then vanish from the Map, but you'll be free to grab some Food at an Inn or seek out easier Traces, saving your Spell Energy for more suitable encounters.

If you decide to have a go at the Confoundable, quickly trace your finger on the screen, following the indicated gesture to cast the appropriate spell. You should begin your spell at the burst of magic, and end the spell at the directional arrow. One point of your **SPELL ENERGY** is consumed with each cast, so a difficult encounter could cost you a fair amount of Spell Energy if it takes you multiple casts to overcome it.

Tracing the gesture quickly and accurately increases the spell's effectiveness, boosting your chances of success. The **SPELL GAUGE** at the top of your screen tells you how well you've performed, either Fair, Good, Great, or Masterful. The more you practice particular spells, the better you'll likely be at casting them in the future!

With a bit of skillful spellcasting and a pinch of luck, you'll succeed in defeating the Confoundable. The Foundable will return to its proper place.

Of course, things don't always go as planned, and sometimes, even the best-cast spells go awry. In the event that your spell fails, you'll lose a bit of **SPELL ENERGY**, shown in the bottom left corner of the screen. You're free to try again, provided you have enough Spell Energy for another cast.

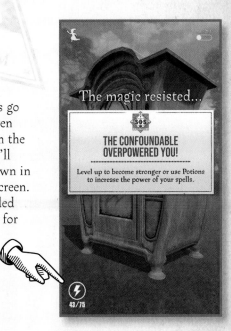

However, Confoundables don't always wait around for you to get it right. A single or series of unfortunate spell casts might cause a Confoundable to **DEPART**, bringing the Encounter to a swift end. The Trace then vanishes from the Map; you'll need to continue your search elsewhere. Not to worry, though; there's always another Trace nearby!

If you really want to return a Foundable you've encountered but feel you might need some help, consider using a **POTION**. Tap the **POTIONS ICON** at the bottom right corner of the screen to open your Suitcase and view your supply. Certain Potions, such as **EXSTIMULO POTION**, can have a dramatic impact on the Encounter, improving your spellcast and boosting your odds of success.

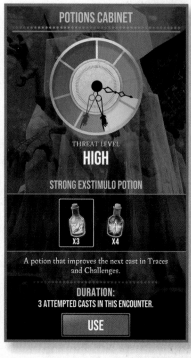

It's a good idea to brew up a few useful Potions before you start tracking down Traces. Turn to p. 64 to learn all about this important process!

Each time you banish a Confoundable and return a Foundable, you're taken to the **REWARDS SUMMARY** screen, which shows a Patronus descending through a series of rewards including a Foundable or a Fragment of the Foundable you've collected; Rank Experience Points, or **RANK XP**, accumulated for the corresponding magical Family in your Registry; and finally, your overall Experience Points, or **XP**. These rewards are provided by the Ministry as thanks for doing your part to protect the wizarding world.

REWARDS SUMMARY

Gobstone Set
1/1

+3   XP
            +320

> Looking for even more rewards? Bonus XP is awarded for succeeding on your first spell cast, for achieving higher levels of casting (i.e., Great or Masterful casts), or for the first time you collect a certain Foundable.

Gobstone Set
+1
Fragments
1/1 MAX

Best of all, you receive a Foundable or a Fragment of a Foundable each time you return a Foundable. This important reward moves you one step closer to completing the **EXPLORATION** part of your **REGISTRY**. Collect enough Foundables and Fragments to complete each **IMAGE** in the Registry, and you'll eventually fill your Registry with Images of every Foundable! Turn to p. 28 to learn all about the Registry and the rewards you'll reap by completing it!

> Eager to see what each Image looks like? If you don't mind these sorts of spoilers, turn to p. 138 for a catalog!

In *Wizards Unite*, the Ministry has provided all S.O.S. Task Force witches and wizards with an important tome known as the **REGISTRY**. Stored in your Suitcase, the Registry is a special book that magically tracks your progress through the game. It keeps a careful record of practically everything you see and do, letting you easily explore all you've accomplished and discover what still needs doing.

The Registry features four Sections: **EXPLORATIONS**, **CHALLENGES**, **MYSTERIES**, and **EVENTS**, which are further divided into **FAMILIES**, which are further divided into **PAGES**. Tap the icons at the bottom of the screen to switch between each Section, then swipe left or right across the screen (or tap the icons near the top) to flip between the current Section's Families. Scroll vertically within each Family to find the individual Pages where the Fragments of your Foundables appear.

Each **REGISTRY PAGE** is blank at first, showing only silhouettes of the Foundables. By returning Foundables, you'll steadily fill in their **IMAGES** on the Registry Pages, completing the Registry. This important log marks your progress in your fight against the Calamity, and is essential to fulfilling your Ministry mission. You'll also reap some excellent rewards in the process!

REGISTRY

EXPLORATIONS

Foundables that can be returned by investigating **Traces** you discover on the Map (p. 140).

- FAMILIES:
Care of Magical Creatures, Dark Arts, Hogwarts School, Legends of Hogwarts, Ministry of Magic, Magizoology, Magical Games and Sports, Mysterious Artifacts, Wonders of the Wizarding World, Oddities

- PAGES:
New pages are being added all the time, so be sure to check your Registry carefully when there's a game update!

CHALLENGES

Foundables that can be returned when you succeed at **Wizarding Challenges** (p. 154).

- FAMILIES:
Books, Deathly Hallows, Hogwarts Register, Horcruxes, Inquisitorial Squad, Joke Products, Magical Devices, Quidditch Teams, Symbols of the Wizarding World, Wands of Dumbledore's Army, Wands of the Order of the Phoenix, Adversary Wanted Posters

- PAGES:
New Pages are being added all the time, so be sure to check your Registry carefully when there's a game update!

MYSTERIES

Foundables that provide clues to the mystery surrounding the **Calamity** (p. 106).

- FAMILIES:
Rather than Families, the Mysteries section of the Registry is divided into Chapters that further the story around the Calamity.

- PAGES:
New Pages are being added all the time, so be sure to check your Registry carefully when there's a game update!

EVENTS

Foundables that can be returned during special Events that occur throughout the year (p. 72).

- FAMILIES:
Dependent upon current or ongoing events

- PAGES:
New Pages are being added all the time, so be sure to check your Registry carefully when there's a game update!

The **FAMILY ICONS** in the Exploration Registry should look quite familiar to you by now. Memorizing the Exploration Family Icons is helpful, as they directly relate to many important items that appear on the Map, such as **TRACES** and **LANDMARKS**. When you're trying to complete a particular Exploration Registry Page, seek out Traces and Landmarks that share the same Family Icon.

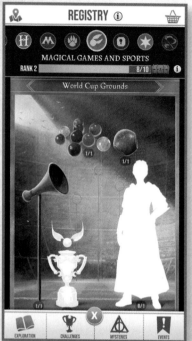

Each time you return a Foundable or complete a Wizarding Challenge, you'll receive a **FRAGMENT** of a Foundable for your Registry. Foundables that feature low **THREAT LEVELS** typically require fewer Fragments to complete their Images, while those of a higher Threat Level require more. The number of Fragments needed to complete each Image is shown at the base of the Image's silhouette on the Registry Page. Or, after an encounter, you can see the number of Fragments required to complete the Image in the Rewards Summary.

Tap any Image silhouette in the Registry to bring up more info on the related Foundable. Naturally, you won't learn much if you've never seen the Foundable or obtained any of its Fragments before, but every little bit of information helps!

Quidditch World Cup

MEDIUM

SEEN: 2   FRAGMENTS : 1

Since 1473 the Quidditch World Cup has been the wizarding world's premier international sporting event. Held every four years, national teams from across the globe battle for the prestigious title of world champions.

RETURNED: FRIDAY, 03 MAY 2019

FOUND AT: SAN FRANCISCO, UNITED STATES

RETURNED TO: INTERNATIONAL CONFEDERATION OF WIZARDS' QUIDDITCH COMMITTEE

X

Once you've seen a Foundable or obtained a Fragment of one, its Registry silhouette gains a bit of color, and more information is displayed when you tap it. This update to the Registry occurs even if you encounter a Foundable but fail to claim its Fragment; the mere act of seeing a Foundable in a Trace Encounter is enough to update its Registry Image accordingly.

Collect the requisite number of Fragments for a Foundable, and its Image will at last materialize on the appropriate Page of the Registry. Now you can tap the Image to learn all about the Foundable, and perhaps even take a **PHOTO** with it!

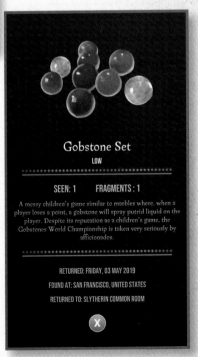

Gobstone Set

LOW

SEEN: 1   FRAGMENTS : 1

A messy children's game similar to marbles where, when a player loses a point, a gobstone will spray putrid liquid on the player. Despite its reputation as a children's game, the Gobstones World Championship is taken very seriously by afficionados.

RETURNED: FRIDAY, 03 MAY 2019

FOUND AT: SAN FRANCISCO, UNITED STATES

RETURNED TO: SLYTHERIN COMMON ROOM

X

Select Foundables can pose for you, letting you snap photos of some of the Wizarding World's most-beloved characters.

Tracking down Foundables and filling out the Registry has even more benefits. Notice the meter near the top of each Registry Family? This is the **FAMILY XP BAR**. Each time you add a Fragment to any Image on a Page, that Page's Family gains some XP. Fill the Family XP Bar by collecting lots of Fragments, and the Family will rank up, gifting you a **TREASURE TRUNK**.

Like the rewards you get for returning a Foundable, you never quite know what a Treasure Trunk will contain, but rest assured its contents will be good! Treasure Trunks commonly provide precious items like **SCROLLS** and **RUNESTONES**, which help you grow as a witch or wizard and enable you to participate in **WIZARDING CHALLENGES** held at Fortresses. Treasure Trunks earned by ranking up Challenge Registry Pages may also contain highly prized **SPELL BOOKS**, which can provide a significant boost to your wizarding skills! Turn to p. 56 for more.

RANK UP

★Magical Games and Sports★

3

RANK

MAGICAL GAMES AND SPORTS TREASURE TRUNK

MAGICAL GAMES AND SPORTS TREASURE TRUNK

+2 SCROLLS

+1 LVL.2 MAGICAL GAMES AND SPORTS RUNESTONE

MYSTERIES REGISTRY

Note that chapters of the Mysteries Section cannot be ranked up. This is because these Fragments are obtained differently from the Exploration, Challenges, and Events Fragments. For more info, flip to p. 102.

★ ODDITIES ★

Not all **TRACES** are what they seem. Ones with a special trace icon indicate the presence of an **ODDITY**, a rare and dangerous type of Trace Encounter that involves **COMBAT**.

Investigate the Trace, but only if you dare, for you'll be drawn into Combat with a dangerous **FOE**! Cast spells to deflect its blows and defeat the Foe, just as you would during a Wizarding Challenge. Drink Potions as needed until you succeed.

Defeating the Oddity earns you special rewards, including a **FRAGMENT** to help you complete your **ODDITY PAGES** (found at the far end of the Exploration Registry). These Registry Pages can be leveled up just like any other, letting you score more precious Treasure Trunks that contain rare prizes!

Oddities on this Registry Page are more likely to appear at night, during certain phases of the moon.

1	CENTAUR BOW
2	WEREWOLF
3	PIXIE
4	VAMPIRE
5	BROWN CENTAUR

Oddities on this Registry Page appear depending on the time of day.

1	LEPRECHAUN
2	ERKLING
3	HORNED SERPENT EGG
4	HORNED SERPENT
5	DOXY

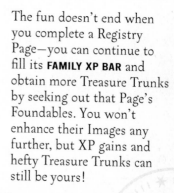

The fun doesn't end when you complete a Registry Page—you can continue to fill its **FAMILY XP BAR** and obtain more Treasure Trunks by seeking out that Page's Foundables. You won't enhance their Images any further, but XP gains and hefty Treasure Trunks can still be yours!

Also, if you so choose, you have the option to **PRESTIGE** a completed Registry Page, enhancing it to new levels, complete with an impressive, upgraded border. Prestiging a Registry Page reverts its Images back to empty silhouettes, so you'll need to venture forth and collect more Fragments to complete the Images again. Fill out a Prestiged Page to Prestige it yet again, scoring an even more elaborate border. See how many times you can Prestige each of your Pages, all the while reaping rewards from Treasure Trunks.

There's a lot going on when it comes to completing the Registry, so let's break things down for clarity:

EXPLORATION ORDER OF OPERATIONS

Explore the world
to find Traces

Successfully complete Trace
Encounters to return Foundables

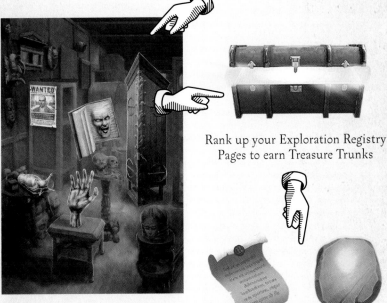

Rank up your Exploration Registry
Pages to earn Treasure Trunks

Return many Foundables to
complete Registry Pages

Use the Scrolls and Runestones
obtained from Treasure Trunks to
advance as a wizard and participate in
Wizarding Challenges

✷ PORTKEYS ✷

Magic is truly all around you in *Harry Potter: Wizards Unite*, and **PORTKEYS** are perhaps the most stunning example of this. By using **KEYS** to unlock **PORTMANTEAUS**, you can use Portkeys to transport you to iconic locations in the wizarding world like never before!

****

Two important items are required to activate
a Portkey: a **PORTMANTEAU**, and a **KEY**.

****

PORTMANTEAUS occasionally pop up on the Map as you explore. Approach and tap them to collect them, just like Potion Ingredients.

The Ministry has provided you with a **GOLD KEY**, which you can use as many times as you like. That said, the Gold Key can only be used in one Portmanteau at a time, so you'll need to unlock the Portmanteau you used it on before using it again.

SILVER KEYS can be acquired as rewards for leveling up or purchased from Wiseacres in Diagon Alley. Silver Keys can be used only once and vanish after the Portmanteau has been unlocked.

Once you've found a Portmanteau, pop open your Suitcase and use a Gold or Silver Key to unlock it. The next part involves a few extra steps—literally! Your Portmanteaus are powered by the distance you travel after using a Key, and some Portmanteaus require you to journey farther than others. The farther you travel, the more likely the resulting Portkey will lead you to someplace rare! Check the Portmanteau in your Suitcase to see how far you've trekked since inserting the Key.

When you've walked the proper distance, you'll receive a notification that your Portkey is ready to place. Open the Portkey menu and tap **PLACE** to set your Portkey. A **PORTKEY PREVIEW** then appears, showing an outline of the area that will serve as the setting for the Portkey. Try to ensure the entire Portkey Preview fits comfortably in your surroundings; spaces like parks, backyards, and living rooms are ideal candidates for Portkey placement.

TAP to place Portkey!

 ATTENTION WIZARDS!

Be very careful when placing Portkeys, and always remain aware of your surroundings. Never place them in dangerous or busy areas such as streets or parking lots!

The Portkey materializes in the selected spot, providing a portal to the wizarding world.

Beyond the portal lies a wizarding world setting filled with vibrant detail. The farther you managed to travel before placing the Portkey, the rarer the location will be!

It's tempting to take your time enjoying the whole Portkey experience, but the journey only lasts for so long. Search your location for **WRACKSPURTS**, the shimmering balls of light swirling about the room. Once you collect five Wrackspurts, you will be taken back to the Map screen.

REWARDS SUMMARY

Goblet of Fire
2/11

+50   XP +50

X

Nabbing every last Wrackspurt nets you special rewards, including rare Fragments for your Registry. Make good use of Portkeys; they'll help you track down rare Foundables and round out your Registry in style.

✶ WRACKSPURTS ✶

While the existence of Wrackspurts has yet to be accepted by the wider wizarding community, Luna Lovegood firmly believes in them. After Harry Potter was stunned by Draco Malfoy during his sixth year at Hogwarts, Luna was able to find him when she used her Spectrespecs to find Wrackspurts swarming about him.

CHAPTER TWO

REALIZE YOUR WIZARD POTENTIAL

> *"It is our choices, Harry, that show what we truly are, far more than our abilities."*
> —Albus Dumbledore

As a witch or wizard with the **STATUTE OF SECRECY TASK FORCE**, the choices you make will impact your journey. Read on to learn how to unlock and hone your magical abilities!

YOUR MINISTRY ID

Issued to you at the very start of your quest, your **MINISTRY ID** is an important document that proves your true identity as a member of the Statute of Secrecy Task Force. All S.O.S. Task Force wizards carry one of these informative cards, which provides a host of progression information in one convenient place.

Tap the various areas of your Ministry ID to start customizing away. You'll unlock new content as you play, letting you personalize your Ministry ID to show off all your in-game successes! Your Ministry ID and Portrait can even be shared online.

Let's take a look at everything you can customize on your Ministry ID:

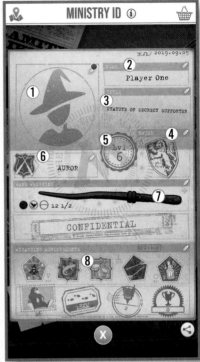

(1) **PHOTO**: Tap here to take a new Ministry ID Portrait then customize it with the many options you unlock as you play. As you know, portraits in the wizarding world capture motion. Using the AR features of the game, your Ministry ID can similarly appear in motion or have other special effects!

(2) **NAME**: Tap here to change your name. The name on your ID is private to you, but you can enter a special tag or name you already have or randomize your name with the click of a button.

(3) **TITLE**: Tap here to choose up to three Titles to show off. You'll unlock new Titles as you earn new achievements.

(4) **HOUSE**: Tap here to choose your Hogwarts House if you already know it. If not, be sure to take the Official Hogwarts House Quiz online and be properly sorted. Adding your Hogwarts House changes the color of your Magical Me.

(5) **WIZARDING LEVEL**: Your current level. Seek out Foundables and Wizarding Challenges to earn XP, level up, and increase your skills.

(6) **PROFESSION**: Once you hit Wizarding Level 6, tap here to choose or change your Profession (p. 52).

(7) **WAND**: Weigh your wand by checking it in with the Ministry. Here you can enter your wand's wood, core, flexibility, and length. If you've never been matched with a wand, take the official quiz online.

(8) **WIZARDING ACHIEVEMENTS**: Tap here to choose up to five Badges to show off with pride.

✳ TITLES AND BADGES ✳

You can earn different **TITLES** and **BADGES** through gameplay, with a different Title or Badge awarded for each achievement.

While some Badges are straightforward to earn, such as opening a certain number of Portkeys or visiting a specific number of Greenhouses, others will require much more effort, including completing many "Masterful" spellcasts or successfully using Protego in combat multiple times.

TITLES	BADGES
WIZARDING WANDERER	
CHALLENGE CHAMPION	
HERBACEOUS HARVESTER	
ADVANCE GUARD	
ACCOMPLISHED ARCHIVIST	
FORTRESS GUARDIAN	
PRACTICED POTIONEER	
DETECTOR COLLECTOR	
PORTKEY PASSENGER	
HELPFUL HERBOLOGIST	
APPRENTICE APOTHECARY	
SUPERIOR SPELLCASTER	
CALAMITY INVESTIGATOR	
ELITE ELIMINATOR	
STRATEGIC SPELLCASTER	
ELIXIR ENTHUSIAST	
S.O.S. AMBASSADOR	
ACCOMPLISHED AUROR	
MASTERFUL MAGIZOOLOGIST	
PROFICIENT PROFESSOR	
DISTINGUISHED DINER	

WIZARDING STATS
(EXPERTISE)

All wizards share twelve common stats that together define their **EXPERTISE**. The higher a wizard's Expertise, the more effective they'll be during **COMBAT ENCOUNTERS** and **WIZARDING CHALLENGES**!

All wizarding stats pertain only to Combat Encounters and Wizarding Challenges. They have no bearing on Exploration, Trace Encounters, or the process of returning Foundables discovered at Traces.

In general, wizarding stats become more important as you advance. It's important to know how each impacts your abilities, since this insight can help you develop advantages around your style of play. No matter which stats you prefer at first, you'll soon realize and appreciate the specific advantages that each one provides.

✳ STAMINA ✳

STAMINA is the amount of damage you can withstand during Combat Encounters. The more Stamina you have, the more hits you can take before being **KNOCKED OUT**. This is an important stat for all wizards who like to go blow-for-blow in Wizarding Challenges. Improve your Expertise in Stamina to withstand more damage when battling **FOES**.

✳ POWER ✳

POWER indicates the amount of damage your spells will inflict on Foes during Combat Encounters. This is a great stat for wizards who like to deal maximum damage with each spell. Spend some effort building Expertise in Power, to take out your opponents quickly and efficiently.

⁂ PROTEGO POWER ⁂

Whenever a Foe attacks you in combat, you're given a brief window to cast **PROTEGO** and defend yourself from the inbound blow. Your Expertise in **PROTEGO POWER** determines how effective your Protego spell will be in reducing the damage from the Foe's attack. Some damage will likely get through, but the greater your Expertise in Protego Power, the less damage you'll take after casting Protego.

⁂ PRECISION ⁂

Wizards with good **PRECISION** have a better chance of landing a **CRITICAL CAST** during Combat Encounters, dealing significant bonus damage. The higher your Precision, the more likely a Critical Cast will occur each time you cast a spell against a Foe.

⁂ CRITICAL POWER ⁂

If a wizard gets lucky and lands a Critical Cast during a Combat Encounter, then their **CRITICAL POWER** stat is used to calculate the extra damage that is dealt. For example, if you have 50 percent Expertise in Critical Power, your spells will deal 50 percent more damage when a Critical Cast occurs. Tip: If you're working at improving your Precision, see if you can increase your Critical Power too!

✳ PROFICIENCY POWER ✳

When you reach **WIZARDING LEVEL 6**, you gain the option to choose a **PROFESSION**, further honing your skill as a wizard. Each Profession has special advantages over certain types of Foes; these advantages are called **PROFICIENCIES**. For example, the **AUROR** Profession has a proficiency against **DARK FORCES**, causing them to deal more damage to Dark Force Foes in Combat. The greater your Expertise in **PROFICIENCY POWER**, the greater your bonus damage will be against the specific types of Foes that are vulnerable to your Profession. (For more about Professions, see p. 52.)

✳ DEFICIENCY DEFENSE ✳

Though choosing a Profession makes you more effective against certain types of Foes, it also makes you vulnerable to other types of Foes. This vulnerability is called a **DEFICIENCY**—and that's where the **DEFICIENCY DEFENSE** stat comes in. Gaining Expertise in Deficiency Defense effectively reduces the Proficiency Power bonus enjoyed by Foes that have a Profession advantage over you. For example, Aurors have a deficiency against **BEASTS**, but if an Auror gains Expertise in Deficiency Defense, Beasts won't be quite as dangerous in battle.

✳ DEFENSE ✳

A straightforward stat, **DEFENSE** simply reduces all incoming damage. The greater your Expertise in Defense, the less damage you'll take during Combat Encounters, sparing your supply of Stamina!

✳ DEFENSE BREACH ✳

Some Foes feature high Expertise in Defense, making them difficult to damage even when you're wielding high Expertise in both Power and Proficiency Power. In these cases, **DEFENSE BREACH** is the stat you need. Increasing your Expertise in Defense Breach effectively reduces your Foes' Defense stat, making Defense-heavy enemies like Werewolves more vulnerable to your attacks.

✳ ACCURACY ✳

Not every Foe will simply stand there and trade blows with you—some are quite evasive and will **DODGE** your spells, costing you precious **SPELL ENERGY** in a fruitless effort. When faced with such slippery Foes, you'll find adding Expertise in **ACCURACY** to be a huge advantage. The greater your Expertise in Accuracy, the more likely your spells will be to find their mark, making it a fine stat for players who enjoy dishing out damage.

As you progress deeper into Wizarding Challenges, you'll soon realize the importance of **STRATEGIC SPELLS**: special hexes and charms you can use outside of Combat to **ENHANCE** allies or **IMPAIR** enemies. These distinct skills can have a dramatic impact on how a Wizarding Challenge unfolds, but they come at a cost: **FOCUS** is required to use a Strategic Spell. That's where the **MAXIMUM FOCUS** stat comes in: the greater your Expertise in this stat, the more Focus you can store, unleashing a series of Strategic Spells at just the right moment!

✴ INITIAL FOCUS ✴

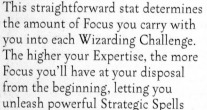

WIZARDING CHALLENGES
Defeat 2 enemies to win!

This straightforward stat determines the amount of Focus you carry with you into each Wizarding Challenge. The higher your Expertise, the more Focus you'll have at your disposal from the beginning, letting you unleash powerful Strategic Spells right from the start.

WIZARD PROFESSIONS

Many witches and wizards are bursting with potential, but your journey accelerates at **WIZARDING LEVEL 6**, when you have the option to choose a **PROFESSION** to specialize in: **AUROR**, **MAGIZOOLOGIST**, or **PROFESSOR**. Each Profession has distinct advantages, so it's a big decision—but don't weigh the choice too heavily; you can easily switch Professions at any time!

As you participate in **WIZARDING CHALLENGES** with friends, one or more of you may wish to switch Professions to achieve a more balanced team. Simply open your Suitcase and tap **PROFESSIONS** to check your progress in each Profession, then tap **SWITCH** to change it. Note that you are unable to switch Professions while engaged in a Challenge, so be sure you know what role you'd like to play beforehand. Having a mixture of Professions is helpful as you delve deeper into Wizarding Challenges, for you'll want the advantages from as many different Professions as possible when facing some of the tougher **FOES**.

Once you've settled on a Profession, you're able to study specific **LESSONS** and grow your Expertise as a wizard. Each Profession has its own **LESSON PLAN**—turn to p. 56 to find out more about them.

> Switching Professions is simple, but it will take longer for you to "max out" your Expertise in a single Profession if you swap often. Experiment with each Profession at first, then pick one to focus on—whichever Profession feels like the right fit for you.

★ AUROR ★

AURORS are Combat veterans who overcome Foes by combining their innate leadership with a litany of debilitating spells. Aurors are most effective against **DARK FORCES**, enjoying a proficiency advantage over such Foes that causes the Auror to deal extra damage equal to their **PROFICIENCY POWER** stat each time an offensive spell lands.

Though all wizards can handle themselves in Combat, none shine quite like Aurors when storming into the fray. Their spells are devastating, designed to send Foes flying with maximum damage. Their Strategic Spells revolve around **IMPAIRING** (weakening) enemies before Combat begins, thereby simplifying the task of defeating them.

Though exceptional at dishing out hexes and damage, Aurors lack the versatility of other Professions. Their Lesson Plan is largely designed to boost their offensive might, making Auror one of the more straightforward Professions to play.

Beware, though: Aurors are vulnerable to **BEASTS**, suffering a deficiency that causes them to take extra damage when attacked by these Foes. This deficiency can be mitigated by learning Lessons that increase the Auror's **DEFICIENCY DEFENSE** stat.

STRATEGIC SPELLS:

	WEAKENING HEX	PLACE AN IMPAIRMENT ON A FOE THAT LOWERS THE FOE'S POWER.
	BAT-BOGEY HEX	REDUCES A FOE'S STAMINA.
	FOCUS CHARM	TRANSFERS YOUR FOCUS TO A TEAMMATE.
	CONFUSION HEX	PLACE AN IMPAIRMENT ON A FOE THAT LOWERS THE FOE'S DEFENSE, DODGE, AND DEFENSE BREACH.

✶ MAGIZOOLOGIST ✶

Trained in the knowledge and care of magical creatures, **MAGIZOOLOGISTS** focus on healing and helping their teammates involved in Combat. When it comes to battling Foes, Magizoologists find themselves quite adept at combating **BEASTS**, dealing bonus damage equal to their **PROFICIENCY POWER** when casting against these Foes.

Magizoologists aren't the heaviest hitters of the three Professions, mind you. Though they have the advantage over Beasts, Magizoologists prefer to **ENHANCE** (heal or empower) allies with a bevy of beneficial **CHARMS**. No other Profession can heal, buff, and even revive fallen allies in the thick of Combat quite like the Magizoologist, lending them a lifesaving support role that every team can benefit from.

Like all Professions, Magizoologists suffer a deficiency against a particular class of Foe: specifically, those that fall into the **CURIOSITIES** category. Magizoologists won't last long in Combat against a Curiosity unless they've devoted some time to boosting their Expertise in their various defensive stats—particularly **DEFICIENCY DEFENSE**.

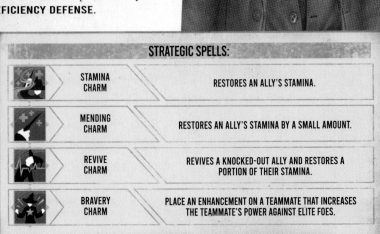

STRATEGIC SPELLS:

	STAMINA CHARM	RESTORES AN ALLY'S STAMINA.
	MENDING CHARM	RESTORES AN ALLY'S STAMINA BY A SMALL AMOUNT.
	REVIVE CHARM	REVIVES A KNOCKED-OUT ALLY AND RESTORES A PORTION OF THEIR STAMINA.
	BRAVERY CHARM	PLACE AN ENHANCEMENT ON A TEAMMATE THAT INCREASES THE TEAMMATE'S POWER AGAINST ELITE FOES.

✴ PROFESSOR ✴

PROFESSORS are highly adept spellcasters who use their deep magical knowledge to debilitate enemies while also supporting their teammates. Professors are most effective when faced with Foes that fall into the **CURIOSITIES** category, as Professors deal extra damage to Curiosities based on their Expertise in **PROFICIENCY POWER**.

Like Magizoologists, Professors often do their best work from the sideline during Wizarding Challenges, devoting their pool of Focus points to unleashing their mighty Strategic Spells. The Professor's toolkit primarily includes charms meant to **IMPAIR** Foes and **ENHANCE** allies, including one that generously buffs the whole team's Proficiency Power. Professors can also unleash a devastating hex that withers away at the Stamina of Foes locked in combat with the Professor's allies.

Of course, Professors also have a weakness against a specific breed of Foe: those that fall under the **DARK FORCES** banner give Professors trouble. Entering into direct Combat against Dark Forces is rarely wise for a Professor—but should the need arise, they'll find great value in boosting their **DEFICIENCY DEFENSE** beforehand.

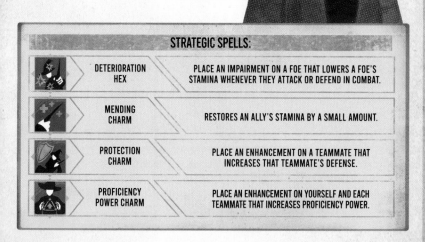

STRATEGIC SPELLS:

	DETERIORATION HEX	PLACE AN IMPAIRMENT ON A FOE THAT LOWERS A FOE'S STAMINA WHENEVER THEY ATTACK OR DEFEND IN COMBAT.
	MENDING CHARM	RESTORES AN ALLY'S STAMINA BY A SMALL AMOUNT.
	PROTECTION CHARM	PLACE AN ENHANCEMENT ON A TEAMMATE THAT INCREASES THAT TEAMMATE'S DEFENSE.
	PROFICIENCY POWER CHARM	PLACE AN ENHANCEMENT ON YOURSELF AND EACH TEAMMATE THAT INCREASES PROFICIENCY POWER.

⚹ LESSON PLANS ⚹

After you've reached **WIZARDING LEVEL 6** and selected a Profession, take a moment to glance at your Profession's **LESSON PLAN**. Each Profession has a unique Lesson Plan filled with special **LESSONS** designed to increase a wizard's **EXPERTISE** in **COMBAT ENCOUNTERS**. Simply spend some of the hard-earned **SCROLLS** and **SPELL BOOKS** you've found in **TREASURE TRUNKS** and Restricted Section Books you've earned during Events. to learn new Lessons, instantly gaining Expertise and unlocking new **PROFESSION BENEFITS** and **STRATEGIC SPELLS** as you go!

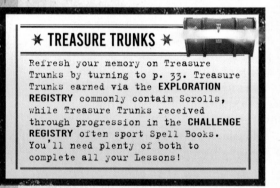

⚹ TREASURE TRUNKS ⚹

Refresh your memory on Treasure Trunks by turning to p. 33. Treasure Trunks earned via the **EXPLORATION REGISTRY** commonly contain Scrolls, while Treasure Trunks received through progression in the **CHALLENGE REGISTRY** often sport Spell Books. You'll need plenty of both to complete all your Lessons!

Tap any Lesson (the little circular nodes) within the Lesson Plan to call up its info. You'll see a brief description, along with the exact Expertise benefits provided by the Lesson. At the bottom of the window you'll see the number of Scrolls, Spell Books, and/or Restricted Section Books it will cost you to learn the Lesson, while your current inventory of Scrolls, Spell Books, and Restricted Section Books is displayed in the top left corner of your screen. Tap the **UPGRADE** button to learn the Lesson, gain its benefits, and unlock the next Lesson on its path within the Lesson Plan.

PLAYING DIRTY

Unlock the previous node to gain access to this upgrade.

DEFENCE VS FOES WITH LESS THAN 50% STAMINA
+10%

CLOSE

Scrolls, Spell Books, and Restricted Section Books are hard to come by, so think carefully before you devote any of yours to learning new Lessons. Tap Lessons that lie farther ahead in your Lesson Plan for a glimpse at what lies down each potential course of study, then plot out your "path through the plan" accordingly. Most Lessons feature multiple upgrades, but you don't need to master each Lesson to unlock the next. Simply learning the first part of the Lesson is enough to open the next one ahead.

Careful study of your Lesson Plan reveals that four unique styles of **ICONS** are used to denote whether each Lesson will simply increase your Expertise stats, or if it's a special Lesson that will unlock a powerful new **PROFESSION BENEFIT** or **STRATEGIC SPELL**. The latter Lessons require more Scrolls, Spell Books, and Restricted Section Books to learn, but they're also among the most valuable Lessons to study, making them well worth the expense.

THE WEAKENING HEX

Harry Potter introduces you to the Weakening Hex, a common tool in the Auror's arsenal. This Hex Impairs Foes by lowering their Power, reducing the damage they can do per cast.

WEAKENING HEX

Impair a Foe by lowering their Power.

UPGRADE
4

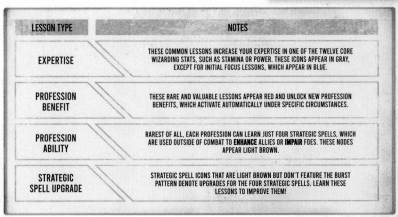

LESSON TYPE	NOTES
EXPERTISE	THESE COMMON LESSONS INCREASE YOUR EXPERTISE IN ONE OF THE TWELVE CORE WIZARDING STATS, SUCH AS STAMINA OR POWER. THESE ICONS APPEAR IN GRAY, EXCEPT FOR INITIAL FOCUS LESSONS, WHICH APPEAR IN BLUE.
PROFESSION BENEFIT	THESE RARE AND VALUABLE LESSONS APPEAR RED AND UNLOCK NEW PROFESSION BENEFITS, WHICH ACTIVATE AUTOMATICALLY UNDER SPECIFIC CIRCUMSTANCES.
PROFESSION ABILITY	RAREST OF ALL, EACH PROFESSION CAN LEARN JUST FOUR STRATEGIC SPELLS, WHICH ARE USED OUTSIDE OF COMBAT TO ENHANCE ALLIES OR IMPAIR FOES. THESE NODES APPEAR LIGHT BROWN.
STRATEGIC SPELL UPGRADE	STRATEGIC SPELL ICONS THAT ARE LIGHT BROWN BUT DON'T FEATURE THE BURST PATTERN DENOTE UPGRADES FOR THE FOUR STRATEGIC SPELLS. LEARN THESE LESSONS TO IMPROVE THEM!

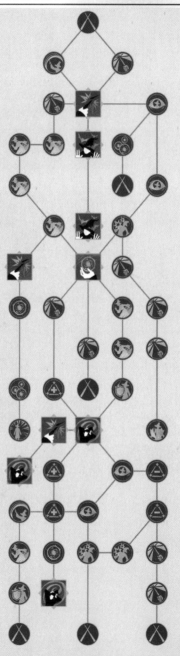

When looking to expand your Expertise as an Auror, look no further than the **AUROR FUNDAMENTALS** Lesson Plan! Here you'll find a straightforward, powerful course of study that's sure to improve your skill as a spellcaster on the front lines of combat.

Spend a moment or two tapping around the Auror's Lessons, and a theme soon emerges: Skill nodes on the left and right sides pertain to increasing stats such as **STAMINA** and **POWER**, while most of the Auror's four **STRATEGIC SPELLS** and their upgrades are found down the central path.

Aurors who start by sticking to the right side of their Lesson Plan will learn more offensive Lessons on **PRECISION** and Power right from the start, improving their ability to breach their Foes' defenses and dish out damage with spells. Those who start off on the left path will increase their Stamina and **PROTEGO POWER**, increasing their own defenses and allowing them to withstand stronger attacks.

The Lesson Plan's central path can be reached at several points from both the right and left paths, and it holds all four of the Auror's Strategic Spell Lessons. You'll want to learn these special Lessons as soon as possible, so keep them in mind when plotting your path through the Auror Fundamentals. The two **PROFESSION BENEFIT** Lessons that lie along the central path provide huge boosts to the Auror's damage against full-Stamina Foes, making their first strike against each more powerful.

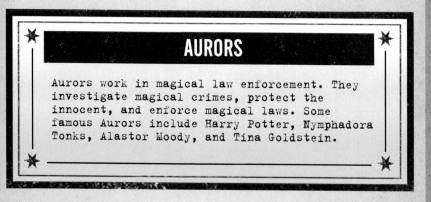

AURORS

Aurors work in magical law enforcement. They investigate magical crimes, protect the innocent, and enforce magical laws. Some famous Aurors include Harry Potter, Nymphadora Tonks, Alastor Moody, and Tina Goldstein.

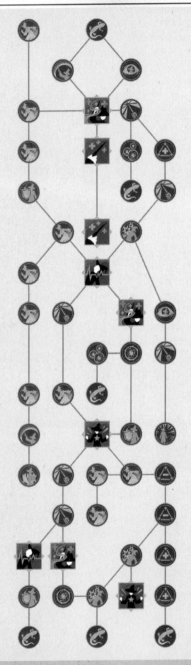

A fascinating Lesson Plan, **FOUNDATIONAL MAGIZOOLOGY** teaches aspiring Magizoologists the basics of proper defense and underscores the importance of sound teamwork. Featuring four **STRATEGIC SPELL** Lessons that focus on healing and restoration, along with an array of **PROFESSIONAL BENEFIT** Lessons that reward the student for maintaining proper **STAMINA** and **FOCUS**, Foundational Magizoology is a fantastic course of study that's sure to appeal to wizards who prioritize safety and support.

The plan's left side is loaded with Lessons that boost the Magizoologist's Expertise in Stamina and Defense. Precious few offensive Lessons are to be found over here. Reach the left path's end to find a few Strategic Spell upgrade Lessons, along with a useful Profession Benefit Lesson that greatly boosts the student's Defense against Snakes.

Venture down the plan's right side to find a sparse selection of offensive Lessons, many of which strengthen less aggressive stats like **PROFICIENCY POWER** and **PRECISION**. The two Profession Benefit Lessons found along the right path increase the Magizoologist's Defense when in good health and provide a significant Power boost when battling Erklings.

Like the Auror's Lesson Plan, the four Strategic Spell Lessons are in Foundational Magizoology's central path, and they are by far the Magizoologist's most important Lessons to learn. In *Wizards Unite*, the Magizoologist's strengths lie in enhancing, healing, and reviving allies.

Should Magizoologists be forced to enter the fray, their plan's two central Profession Benefit Lessons become of great value. Each provides a massive boost to the Magizoologist's Combat capability when five or more points of Focus are stored up. This puts an emphasis on conserving Focus until the need to rescue allies becomes dire!

MAGIZOOLOGISTS

Magizoologists study, rescue, and support the care of magical creatures such as unicorns, dragons, and Nifflers. Famous Magizoologists include Rubeus Hagrid and Newt Scamander, the author of *Fantastic Beasts and Where to Find Them*.

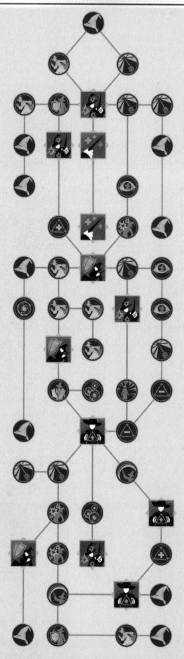

PRINCIPLES OF PROFESSORSHIP provides an excellent Lesson Plan that all aspiring Professors would do well to study. Indeed, its very first **STRATEGIC SPELL** Lesson teaches students the devastating Deterioration Hex, which reduces the afflicted Foe's Stamina each time they attack or defend themselves in Combat.

Hexing enemies has its benefits, since many of the **PROFESSION BENEFIT** Lessons found within the Professor's Lesson Plan teach them to become more effective in Combat against hexed Foes. These Lessons are all found along the plan's left side, and they pair wonderfully with the many hexes that allied Aurors might employ.

It's not all hexes for the Professor. This Lesson Plan primarily teaches **CHARMS**, supportive Strategic Spells that let the Professor heal and **ENHANCE** their frontline allies. The Magizoologist holds top prize as team healer and reviver, yet the Professor has an important role to play as well: Enhancing their allies' **DEFENSES** to keep them from needing much healing!

Speaking of Enhancing allies, the Profession Benefit Lessons found on the right side of the Professor's plan grant extra benefits to the Professor whenever they're buffed. This makes Professors especially dangerous, especially when combined in the Challenge arena with other Professors and Magizoologists.

PROFESSORS

Professors are masters of their chosen field, hired to help mold students into capable wizards, but also responsible for furthering the study of their field. Famous professors include Albus Dumbledore, Minerva McGonagall, Pomona Sprout, and Severus Snape.

BREWING POTIONS

"For those select few who possess the predisposition, I can teach you how to bewitch the mind and ensnare the senses. I can tell you how to bottle fame, brew glory, and even put a stopper in death."

—*Severus Snape*

It's not long into your career as an S.O.S. Task Force wizard before you discover the many advantages that **POTIONS** provide. Potions are specially brewed to bestow benefits to the consumer. Whether you're exploring the **MAP**, facing off against **CONFOUNDABLES**, or preparing to storm a **FORTRESS** with fellow witches and wizards, you'll always benefit from having plenty of Potions on hand.

Potions can be earned as rewards when you level up, and in a pinch, they can also be purchased on demand from **DIAGON ALLEY**. This is how you'll procure Potions until you hit **WIZARDING LEVEL 4**, when you gain the ability to **BREW** Potions on your own. You'll likely hit Level 4 fairly quickly in your exploits, at which point your purchased and rewarded Potions can simply supplement your existing stores.

Before you can brew Potions, you'll first need to gather some **INGREDIENTS**. These special components appear all around you as you explore the Map; tap them to stuff them into your **SUITCASE**. **GREENHOUSES** also serve as reliable sources of many Ingredients as well; find a few that are easy to reach and frequent them when you need to stock up.

✳ POTION INGREDIENTS ✳

POTION INGREDIENTS come in all shapes and sizes, and some Ingredients are easier to find than others. Certain Ingredients appear more abundantly during special conditions, like when it's raining. Below are the twenty-seven unique Ingredients used to brew Potions, and what you can make with them.

INGREDIENT	NAME	DESCRIPTION
	ABRAXAN HAIR	AN INGREDIENT IN STRONG EXSTIMULO POTION, SUBSTITUTED FOR THE WEAKER GRANIAN HAIR. PULLED FROM THE MANE OF A WINGED ABRAXAN MARE.
	ARMADILLO BILE	AN INGREDIENT IN WIT-SHARPENING POTION, WITH A REMARKABLY PUTRID SCENT.
	BITTER ROOT	A PRIMARY INGREDIENT IN ALL VARIATIONS OF EXSTIMULO POTION. GROWN INSIDE A GREENHOUSE.
	BUBOTUBER PUS	AN ESSENTIAL INGREDIENT IN HEALING POTION, SQUEEZED FROM THE PUSTULES OF THE BUBOTUBER PLANT.
	BUTTER-SCOTCH	A KEY INGREDIENT IN DAWDLE DRAUGHT, LENDING AN ALLURING, SWEET SCENT TO THE POTION'S FUMES.
	DRAGON LIVER	A POWERFUL INGREDIENT, ESSENTIAL FOR THE BREWING OF HEALING POTION, BUT VERY RARE AND DIFFICULT TO OBTAIN.
	POWDERED DRAGON CLAW	AN INGREDIENT IN BARUFFIO'S BRAIN ELIXIR, A POTION SAID TO BRING ON CLEVERNESS.
	ESSENCE OF DITTANY	A STANDARD INGREDIENT IN HEALING POTION, RENOWNED FOR ITS REJUVENATING PROPERTIES.
	FROG BRAIN	AN UNPLEASANT BUT NECESSARY INGREDIENT IN BARUFFIO'S BRAIN ELIXIR.
	GINGER ROOT	A VERSATILE POTION-MAKING INGREDIENT USED IN WIT-SHARPENING POTION.

INGREDIENT	NAME	DESCRIPTION
	GRANIAN HAIR	AN INGREDIENT IN EXSTIMULO POTIONS, PULLED FROM THE TAIL OF A MAGNIFICENT WINGED STALLION.
	GROUND SCARAB BEETLES	A KEY INGREDIENT IN WIT-SHARPENING POTION, MADE FROM THE CRUSHED CARAPACES OF SCARAB BEETLES.
	HERMIT CRAB SHELL	AN INGREDIENT IN DAWDLE DRAUGHT THAT INSTILLS A SENSE OF SECURITY AND HOMINESS.
	HONEYWATER	A STANDARD INGREDIENT IN ALL VARIATIONS OF INVIGORATION DRAUGHT.
	LEAPING TOADSTOOL	AN ESSENTIAL INGREDIENT IN BARUFFIO'S BRAIN ELIXIR, MORE DIFFICULT TO CHOP THAN ITS NON-LEAPING COUNTERPART.
	LOVAGE	USED IN INVIGORATION DRAUGHT.
	NEWT SPLEEN	A PARTICULARLY SLIMY INGREDIENT IN WIT-SHARPENING POTION.
	RE'EM BLOOD	USED IN THE RECIPE FOR ALL VARIATIONS OF EXSTIMULO POTION.
	RUNESPOOR EGGS	A POTION-MAKING INGREDIENT KNOWN TO INCREASE MENTAL AGILITY, USED IN THE BREWING OF BARUFFIO'S BRAIN ELIXIR.
	SCURVYGRASS	A STANDARD INGREDIENT USED IN THE BREWING OF ALL VARIATIONS OF INVIGORATION DRAUGHT.
	SNEEZEWORT	USED IN STRONG INVIGORATION DRAUGHT.
	SNOWDROP	A KEY INGREDIENT IN EXSTIMULO POTIONS, KNOWN FOR ITS RESILIENCE.
	SOPOPHOROUS BEAN	USED IN THE BREWING OF DAWDLE DRAUGHT, DUE TO ITS SLEEP-INDUCING PROPERTIES.
	UNICORN HAIR	A POWERFUL ITEM USED IN WANDS AND POTIONS. SUBSTITUTED FOR THE WEAKER ABRAXAN HAIR IN THE POTENT EXSTIMULO POTION.
	VALERIAN ROOT	A KEY ELEMENT OF DAWDLE DRAUGHT, KNOWN FOR ITS SEDATIVE PROPERTIES.
	VERVAIN INFUSION	USED IN THE BREWING OF ALL VARIATIONS OF INVIGORATION DRAUGHT.
	WORMWOOD	AN ESSENTIAL INGREDIENT FOR HEALING POTION.

✶ THE POTIONS BENCH ✶

When you're ready to start brewing, the **POTIONS BENCH** is the place to be! Reach **WIZARDING LEVEL 4** to unlock the Potions Bench, then open your Suitcase to find it there, ready and waiting for you to brew.

Begin by tapping the **BREW NOW** button at the bottom of the screen to open your **RECIPES**. Tap the lowercase **i** icon next to each Potion in the Recipes to call up its full description. Pick the Potion you'd like to create, then tap the big **BREW** button next to it to add it to the brewing queue. Up to four Potions can be queued for brewing, with each one brewing automatically after the other. For each potion, you will see how many ingredients you have in your Vault as well as how many are needed to begin brewing. If you are missing ingredients to create the potion, the Brew button will read "Get Missing," along with the cost of buying the missing ingredients. By clicking this button, you can trade Gold for the required ingredients and start brewing.

Only a few recipes are available at first, but you'll eventually learn more as you advance your Wizarding Level. You'll also unlock another **CAULDRON,** letting you queue up even more Potions for a small cost.

✷ MASTER NOTES ✷

POTIONS

Brewing **POTIONS** takes a bit of time, but wizards can quicken the process by discovering each Potion's **MASTER NOTES**. Tap the ladle resting in your bubbling **CAULDRON** while a Potion is brewing to give it a try. Perform a few skillful stirs, and you'll greatly hasten the Potion's brewing time, letting you bottle lots of Potions much faster.

Each recipe's Master Notes are unknown to you at first—you will need to discover them. Tap the lowercase **i** icon at the top of the screen to bring up the complete list of **GESTURES** you can perform to stir the cauldron. Experiment with different combinations of these Gestures as your Potion brews. Should you guess all the right stirs in their proper order, the Master Notes will take effect, and you'll acquire the completed potion!

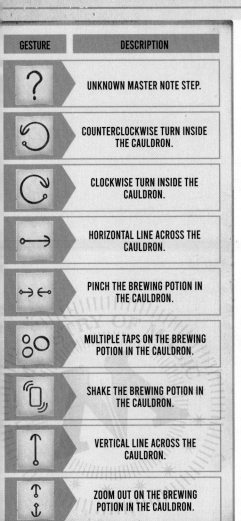

GESTURE	DESCRIPTION
?	UNKNOWN MASTER NOTE STEP.
↺	COUNTERCLOCKWISE TURN INSIDE THE CAULDRON.
↻	CLOCKWISE TURN INSIDE THE CAULDRON.
→•	HORIZONTAL LINE ACROSS THE CAULDRON.
→←•	PINCH THE BREWING POTION IN THE CAULDRON.
○○	MULTIPLE TAPS ON THE BREWING POTION IN THE CAULDRON.
📱	SHAKE THE BREWING POTION IN THE CAULDRON.
↑	VERTICAL LINE ACROSS THE CAULDRON.
↑⚓	ZOOM OUT ON THE BREWING POTION IN THE CAULDRON.

Repeat this process and perform a Potion's Master Notes **THREE TIMES** to memorize it. You'll then copy down the Master Notes on the Potion's page in your Recipes, preserved for future reference. Master Notes can only be performed once on each potion brew to reduce your brew time.

EXSTIMULO POTION

🔲 x1

Improves your spellcast in both combat and Traces.

🌻	🦪	🌾	🐌
10/1	11/1	12/1	9/1

⏱ 1H 0M

MASTER NOTES

REDUCE BREWING TIME BY 9M 0S

↑ •↑• ↻

ⓧ

POTION PERFECTION

Professor Severus Snape, who served as Hogwarts Potions Master, was incredibly gifted at potion-making from a young age. He recorded his observations in his copy of *Advanced Potion-Making*, which fell into the possession of Harry Potter during his sixth-year Potions class. Harry quickly became a much more accomplished Potions student with the help of Snape's insights.

Need to brew even faster? In a pinch, you can click the green Finish button in the bottom left corner of the screen to exchange Gold for speeding up brewing.

POTIONS

Now that you know how to brew **POTIONS**, let's take a closer look at each of the unique Potions available to you for brewing.

✳ EXSTIMULO POTION ✳

The **EXSTIMULO POTION** empowers your next three spell casts in both Trace and **WIZARDING CHALLENGES**. It effectively makes returning Foundables easier by enhancing your spellcasting ability, and also makes defeating Foes in Combat easier by **ENHANCING** your **POWER**.

WIZARDING LEVEL: 4
INGREDIENTS: Bitter Root, Re'em Blood, Snowdrop, Granian Hair

✳ STRONG EXSTIMULO POTION ✳

As its name implies, the **STRONG EXSTIMULO POTION** is a more effective version of its standard Exstimulo Potion peer. It has a much greater effect on your spellcasting ability with Foundables and your Power against Foes on your next fourcasts. Brewing takes much longer though, so try to queue these up well in advance of needing them.

WIZARDING LEVEL: 7
INGREDIENTS: Bitter Root, Re'em Blood, Snowdrop, Abraxan Hair

✳ POTENT EXSTIMULO POTION ✳

The most effective version of the Exstimulo Potion is the **POTENT** variety. It extremely boosts your chances of success in any reasonable Trace or Combat Encounterfor five spell casts, but because it packs a hefty six-hour brewing time, you'll want to queue a few of these up before bed and brew while you snooze.

WIZARDING LEVEL: 9
INGREDIENTS: Bitter Root, Re'em Blood, Snowdrop, Unicorn Hair

✳ BARUFFIO'S BRAIN ELIXIR ✳

It may have the longest brewing time of them all, but **BARUFFIO'S BRAIN ELIXIR** is one of the most useful Potions in the game. Use this Potion to gain double **XP** from each Trace, Portkey, and Wizarding Challenge you successfully complete as you explore. The effect lasts for a full thirty minutes, so you have plenty of time to get out there and boost your Wizarding Level. Just be sure to brew a batch far ahead of when you might need it.

WIZARDING LEVEL: 4
INGREDIENTS: Frog Brain, Runespoor Eggs, Leaping Toadstool, Powdered Dragon Claw

✳ HEALING POTION ✳

Wizards who enjoy the thrill of Combat and Wizarding Challenges know the value of **HEALING POTIONS**. Healing Potions can be consumed to restore a significant amount of your **STAMINA**. Always keep some on hand.

WIZARDING LEVEL: 6
INGREDIENTS: Wormwood, Bubotuber Pus, Essence of Dittany, Dragon Liver

✳ WIT-SHARPENING POTION ✳

Another excellent Potion for Fortress-frequentingwizards the **WIT-SHARPENING POTION** is carefully crafted to improve your spells' effectiveness against the **ELITE FOES** that lurk in the later stages of Wizarding Challenges. Each requires a while to brew, so queue up a supply well in advance of your next Fortress visit.

WIZARDING LEVEL: 15
INGREDIENTS: Newt Spleen, Ginger Root, Ground Scarab Beetles, Armadillo Bile

✳ DAWDLE DRAUGHT ✳

Foundables with high Threat Levels can **DEPART** after a failed spell cast or two. If you fear a Foundable might Depart, try some **DAWDLE DRAUGHT**—brewed to reduce the likelihood of fleeing.

WIZARDING LEVEL: 17
INGREDIENTS: Valerian Root, Sopophorous Bean, Butterscotch, Hermit Crab Shell

✳ INVIGORATION DRAUGHT ✳

Wizards preparing to tackle a difficult Wizarding Challenge will want to bring along this handy Potion, which grants **FOCUS** for Strategic Spells in Wizarding Challenges.

WIZARDING LEVEL: 8
INGREDIENTS: Honeywater, Vervain Infusion, Scurvygrass, and Lovage

✳ STRONG INVIGORATION DRAUGHT ✳

A stronger version of the **INVIGORATION DRAUGHT**, this Potion grants significant Focus for Strategic Spells in Wizarding Challenges and reduces ability cooldown.

WIZARDING LEVEL: 13
INGREDIENTS: Honeywater, Vervain Infusion, Scurvygrass, Lovage, Sneezewort

CHAPTER THREE

EXTRAORDINARY EVENTS

> *"Happiness can be found even in the darkest of times, if one only remembers to turn on the light."*
>
> —Albus Dumbledore

Tracking down Foundables, fighting your way through Wizarding Challenges, and brewing potions isn't all you'll experience in *Harry Potter: Wizards Unite*. Indeed, there is plenty for you to do to help the Ministry contain the **CALAMITY**, from simple everyday tasks to special **EVENTS** that occur throughout the year. Let's explore some of the most exciting Events you can participate in—and the many goodies you'll get when you do!

DAILY ASSIGNMENTS

We'll start with the small stuff and work our way up. First on the list: **ASSIGNMENTS**. The Ministry likes to keep you busy, so they've prepared some special tasks for you to work on each day.

✴ DAILY TREASURE ✴

When you play *Wizards Unite*, you're eligible to receive **DAILY TREASURE**. Simply logging in each day is enough to earn the reward, which could be something as simple as free XP or Spell Energy, or it might be something *really nice*, like a few Scrolls or some Potions. You can't make up any day you missed to earn a Daily Treasure, so make the effort to check in each day.

✶ DAILY ASSIGNMENTS ✶

The Ministry has other goodies for you as well, but these ones require a bit more effort on your part. Tap the **ASSIGNMENTS** button in the bottom right corner of your screen to browse your list of **DAILY TASKS**. The Ministry sends you the same list every day of several small, manageable goals that you can achieve fairly easily. For completing each task, you receive a small **REWARD**, such as Scrolls, Spell Energy, or Potions Ingredients.

IN A TYPICAL DAY, YOU'LL BE ASKED TO:

1. Return ten Foundables.
2. Pick up one Ingredient or Portmanteau.
3. Collect from two Inns.
4. Brew one Potion.
5. Complete all Daily Tasks.
6. And more!

Clearing all Daily Tasks earns you a new bonus: You're then able to complete the final Daily Task, which simply asks you to complete the other tasks. Collect this last Daily Task's reward for additional **GOLD**, then visit Diagon Alley to see what's worth buying.

Completing the sixth and final task also earns you a special certificate commemorating your accomplishment. Collecting rewards each day can quickly add up: Potions, XP, Ingredients, and Gold will get you valuable resources to help you stay one step ahead of the Calamity and advance faster in your Wizarding Challenges.

ACHIEVEMENTS

Hogwarts wasn't built in a day and some tasks take time to complete too. Achievements are tasks that help you show off your dedication and how great a wizard you are. And you get rewards for completing them. The best rewards are Achievement Badges and Titles that you can use to customize your Ministry ID. Achievements are also great if you are uncertain of what to do to help advance the cause of the S.O.S. Taskforce—find an achievement that looks interesting to you and get to work!

✳ EVENTS AND SPECIAL ASSIGNMENTS ✳

The life of a wizard is sure to be filled with magical moments, and some of the most exciting happen during **EVENTS**. These happenings occur regularly throughout the year, often at times that hold a special significance to the **CALAMITY**. During these Events, the Ministry doles out Special Assignments that, once completed, will earn you **RESTRICTED SECTION BOOKS**, unique Registry stickers, and even Lenses, Frames, and Stickers for your Ministry ID Portrait. Unlike Daily Tasks, **SPECIAL ASSIGNMENTS** are ongoing affairs that can be enjoyed for days on end—right up until the Event's scheduled time frame is over.

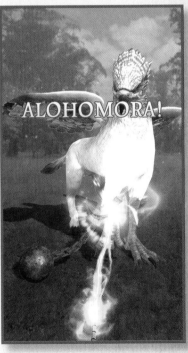

During these events, watch for special traces of magic on the Map, marked by a purple beam emanating from them. The Foundables you will encounter are quite familiar, but have a **BRILLIANT** glow to them. You can collect Registry stickers for these **BRILLIANT FOUNDABLES** in the Event portion of the Registry. To complete the Event pages, you'll have to return these Brilliant Foundables, complete Special Assignments, use Brilliant Runes in Wizarding Challenges, and even open special event Portkeys.

When a **BRILLIANT EVENT** is going on, you can learn more about it by checking your Registry. Tap the **EVENTS INFO** button on the bottom right to call up information on the Event and view any special Registry Pages associated with it. Now that you know a Brilliant Event is occurring, keep an eye on the Map for anything that's projecting a purple beam of light.

Each Event introduces fresh content like new short storylines as well as new Traces, Oddities, or Wizarding Challenges, so you never quite know what's in store. Investigate everything you see during a Brilliant Event to discover new Foundables and battle unique Foes while the chance permits!

CHAPTER FOUR

WIZARDS UNITE!

> *"It is important to fight and fight again, and keep fighting, for only then can evil be kept at bay though never quite eradicated."*
>
> —Albus Dumbledore

Looking for new trials to conquer beyond brewing Potions, charging your Portkeys, and seeking out Traces? Why not team up with some friends and take on a **WIZARDING CHALLENGE**? Though not without their share of risk, Wizarding Challenges are by far the most exciting trials a wizard can face, for it is here that most **COMBAT** encounters occur. The many trials that await you within Wizarding Challenges are best overcome by working together with other S.O.S. Task Force members, and the special rewards you'll receive upon your victory will expand your skill as a wizard and help you complete your **CHALLENGE REGISTRY**. Unite with fellow wizards and tackle new **FOES** to earn rewards in Wizarding Challenges!

As a reminder, all Wizarding Challenges are held at **FORTRESSES**: rare, towering structures that are easy to spot on your Map from afar. Seek out Fortresses in places where people gather for the best chance to team up against **FOES**.

Hurry to any Fortress you see that's surrounded by swirling energy, because this means that other wizards are battling through Challenges there. Tackling Fortresses on your own is extremely dangerous, so unite with the friendly wizards you meet near Fortresses, uniting to tackle the thrilling Challenges that await within.

Up to five wizards can attempt a Wizarding Challenge at once. If your friends are busy, you can still team up with other wizards—you'll automatically be queued with others in the Fortress and sent to a lobby. In the game you'll be able to coordinate and work together to improve your chances of victory!

✶ CHAMBER OF CHAMBERS ✶

Just inside each Fortress lies the **CHAMBER OF CHAMBERS**. This unique entry room connects to each of the Fortress's twenty *other* chambers, which are filled with dangerous **FOES**. You must clear each Foe-filled chamber in sequence to unlock the next one ahead, increasing your likelihood of encountering even more deadly **ELITE FOES**.

Tackling a Challenge with friends? Make sure you all select the same chamber, and try to do so at the same time—this increases your odds of being grouped together!

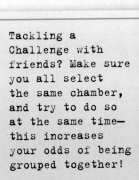

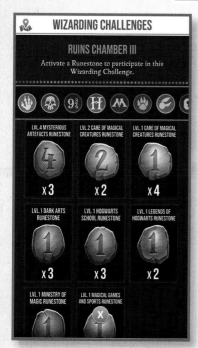

After you've chosen a chamber, the next step is to set your **RUNESTONE**. These rare prizes are found inside the **TREASURE TRUNKS** you receive by returning Foundables and ranking up the **REGISTRY**. All wizards participating must use a Runestone to unlock the **CHALLENGE**. The family and level of the Runestone you choose affects the rewards for the upcoming Challenge, so choose wisely! If you're just starting out, it's best to use low-level Runestones while you get used to the mechanics of combat.

Once all wizards have set a Runestone, simply sit back and wait for the timer to tick down. If you wish to abandon the Challenge, do so before the timer reaches zero, for at that point your Runestones are consumed and the Wizarding Challenge officially begins. You will enter the **ARENA**, where **COMBAT** awaits.

★ THE ARENA ★

Welcome to the **ARENA**! Time is against you here, for you have only a handful of minutes in which to defeat the many **FOES** you face. Take stock of their numbers quickly, then coordinate with your teammates to devise a plan for victory. **COMBAT** begins after you've chosen a Foe to engage!

LEAVE BUTTON

Tap this if you wish to forfeit your **RUNESTONE** and flee the challenge.

CHALLENGE CLOCK

You fail if you run out of time before all enemies are defeated!

THE NUMBER OF FOES DEFEATED

Your progress toward victory!

CHALLENGE TEAM

Each teammate's icon shows their current status and **STAMINA**.

FOE ICONS

These show the Foe's **RANK**, **AFFINITY**, and current status and **STAMINA**.

STRATEGIC SPELL TRAY

Tap one of your **STRATEGIC SPELLS** to use it.

FOCUS METER

Shows how much **FOCUS** you have and how much you can store.

✳ SELECTING A TARGET ✳

Wise wizards know to survey the enemy ranks before rushing headlong into battle. The **FOE ICONS** you see around the Arena provide invaluable info at a glance, helping you pick the perfect Foes to attack. Any Foe Icons that feature green + icons are primary targets, for your chosen **PROFESSION** boasts a proficiency advantage over such Foes.

Tap a Foe Icon to view its name and detailed status, including any special buffs or de-buffs the Foe might feature. If the Foe seems like a favorable matchup, tap the **START** button to enter **COMBAT**.

⋆ ATTACKING! ⋆

The real action begins after you've chosen a **FOE**, for the scene shifts to an up-close view of the selected enemy. **COMBAT** has officially begun!

⋆ CASTING SPELLS ⋆

Quickly touch and control your **WAND**, then drag your cursor onto the circular **TARGET** that appears on the Foe. Do your best to move in sync with the Foe, keeping your cursor over the target as the Foe moves about. Watch the **BLUE LINE** steadily wrap around your circular cursor as you hold it over the Foe's target.

After the blue coloring completes its journey around your cursor, a spell gesture appears onscreen. Trace that pattern as quickly and accurately as you can to unleash a powerful spell that damages the Foe, reducing its **STAMINA**!

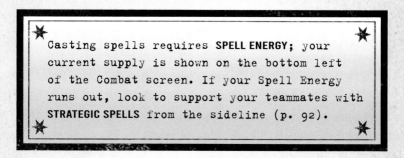

Casting spells requires **SPELL ENERGY**; your current supply is shown on the bottom left of the Combat screen. If your Spell Energy runs out, look to support your teammates with **STRATEGIC SPELLS** from the sideline (p. 92).

Of course, **FOES** won't just sit there and while you attack them. Taking advantage of every opportunity to reduce your Foe's **STAMINA** is important, because you never know when they will strike. Lashing out with attacks of their own means you will have to defend instead of attack!

When a Foe rears back to strike, you have a fleeting moment to cast **PROTEGO** and shield yourself with protective magic. Swipe your screen to cast the spell, but beware that Protego may not fully protect you from harm—some of the Foe's attack damage may still penetrate your shield. Even a poor casting of Protego beats suffering the full brunt of a wrathful attack, so study **LESSONS** that increase your **EXPERTISE** in **PROTEGO POWER** and be ready to swipe your screen at a moment's notice!

PROTEGO

Commonly known as the Shield Charm, Protego casts a protective shield that blocks spells and physical forces. A stronger version of the charm, Protego Maxima, was employed during the Second Wizarding War to shield Hogwarts when Lord Voldemort's forces rallied at its gates. Another variation of the charm, Protego Diabolica, was used by Grindelwald during his 1927 rally in Paris; only those loyal to him could pass through its protective ring of flames unharmed.

✳ USING POTIONS ✳

Should you suffer significant damage and your **STAMINA** begins to dwindle, you may want to make use of a **POTION** or two to help even the odds. **HEALING POTIONS** are fantastic for use during Combat, as they immediately restore a significant amount of your missing Stamina when consumed. If you're fresh out of Potions, don't hesitate to call out to a teammate for healing. You can drink a Potion in Combat or in the Arena. Drinking a Potion in the Arena allows you to respond more quickly or form a plan before engaging your next Foe.

POTIONS CABINET

EXSTIMULO POTION

X8   X6   X4   X7

A potion that slightly improves the next cast in Traces and Challenges.

DURATION:
3 ATTEMPTED CASTS IN THIS ENCOUNTER.

USE

Other Potions can increase your Combat prowess in different ways. The **EXSTIMULO POTIONS** improve your damage by boosting your **POWER**, just the thing for lending your spells some extra sizzle.

✶ GETTING KO'D ✶

Even the most gifted wizards sometimes find themselves overwhelmed. Remember, you can always leave the Encounter by tapping the **LEAVE** button in the upper right corner of the **COMBAT** screen. Should the worst occur and you run completely out of Stamina during Combat, the Combat scenario ends and the scene shifts back to the **ARENA**.

A penalty timer appears if the Foe knocks you out, counting down twenty-five seconds—the "time out" you must endure before returning to the fray. Your **STAMINA** is fully restored after the twenty-five seconds are up, giving you a fighting chance to challenge the Foe once more.

> Depending on how much time is left on the **CHALLENGE CLOCK**, twenty-five seconds might not be all that much of a penalty. You're restored to full Stamina when the penalty expires, so consider whether it's worth drinking a Healing Potion when you could simply wait out the twenty-five seconds required.

✳ CHALLENGE REWARDS ✳

Continue trading blows with your Foe, punishing it with spells and protecting yourself with Protego. Keep it up until you've depleted the Foe's **STAMINA**, then select your next opponent. If all remaining Foes are spoken for, help your allies from the sideline by unleashing powerful **STRATEGIC SPELLS!**

Defeat every Foe within the time limit to secure your victory. You're then granted several rewards, including **FRAGMENTS** for your **CHALLENGE REGISTRY** and rare **SPELL BOOKS** that will help you learn advanced **LESSONS**. Best of all, the Fortress's next chamber becomes unlocked . . . are you ready for what lies ahead?

Many Foes look alike, but appearances can be deceiving. Heed each Foe's name when you tap their **FOE ICONS** in the Arena, for those adorned with **TITLES** pose a far greater threat. You'll encounter more of these **ELITE FOES** as you delve deeper through the Fortress's chambers. If you're playing with friends, be sure to warn them whenever you've found such a Foe, and decide carefully on how to approach it. It's often wise to work together as a group, devoting all resources to bringing down these dangerous threats. **IMPAIR** them with **STRATEGIC SPELLS** and **ENHANCE** whichever ally chooses to face them in Combat. Turn the page to learn more.

ELITE FOE DESCRIPTIONS

Here's the complete list of Foe titles, from least threatening to most:

1. Common
2. Formidable
3. Imposing
4. Dangerous
5. Fierce
6. Elite

✴ STRATEGIC SPELLS ✴

Remember those **STRATEGIC SPELLS** discussed in Chapter 2? Once you've chosen your **PROFESSION** (Auror, Magizoologist, or Professor) and started making your way through your Lesson Plan, you'll notice some unique Lessons in the Plan. These are your Strategic Spells, which you can use outside of **COMBAT** to **ENHANCE** (charm) allies or **IMPAIR** (hex) Foes. Each Profession has four Strategic Spells, with their own strengths in team-based combat.

THE WEAKENING HEX

Harry Potter introduces you to the Weakening Hex, a
common tool in the Auror's arsenal. This Hex Impairs
Foes by lowering their Power, reducing the damage
they can do per cast.

WEAKENING HEX

Impair a Foe by lowering
their Power.

UPGRADE
4

To learn a Strategic Spell, open
your **SUITCASE** and tap **PROFESSION**,
then tap over to your current
LESSON PLAN. Spend the Scrolls,
Spell Books, and Restricted Section
Books you find in **TREASURE TRUNKS**
to learn the **LESSONS** in the Plan.
As you go, look for Lessons with
brown coloring and a burst pattern
around them. Learning each of
these four Lessons unlocks your
four Strategic Spells!

Once you've learned a Strategic
Spell, you're ready to use it in a
CHALLENGE. Unlike spells, Strategic
Spells can only be used in the
ARENA while outside of Combat. To
use a Strategic Spell, simply tap its
icon on the bottom of the screen,
then drag your finger to the desired
target. If the Ability is a **CHARM**,
you'll want to target an ally. If it's
a **HEX**, you'll want to target a Foe.

FOCUS ON THIS

FOCUS is required to use Strategic Spells.
Your current Focus is shown on the **FOCUS METER** near
the bottom of the screen. Earn more Focus by defeating
Foes marked with **FOCUS ICONS**, like the one shown here.
Focus earned in this manner is bestowed to the entire
team, making these Foes valuable targets.

AUROR ABILITIES

Aurors are all about **COMBAT**, and as such, their four **STRATEGIC SPELLS** are meant to primarily **IMPAIR** their **FOES**. Even the most fearsome Foe is easier to face after its been saddled with a slew of debilitating hexes, so unleash as many as possible to gain the advantage going into each fight.

✴ WEAKENING HEX ✴

LOWERS A FOE'S POWER.

The **WEAKENING HEX** is right up an Auror's alley. This special hex **IMPAIRS** its victim by lowering the Foe's **POWER**, causing the Foe to deal less damage with each blow. An excellent hex to employ against any threat, it's especially effective at taking the sting out of heavy hitters. This Strategic Spell can be augmented by two additional Lessons, "Improved Weakness Hex" and "Weakness Hex Maxima," allowing you to impair an enemy's Power by up to 15-30 percent!

✴ BAT-BOGEY HEX ✴

REDUCES A FOE'S STAMINA.

In advance of engaging your next Foe in Combat, consider sapping away some of their **STAMINA** with a blast of the Auror's **BAT-BOGEY HEX**. Less Stamina means fewer spell casts before the Foe is fried! This ability can be upgraded by one additional Lesson, which, when maxed out, reduces an enemy's Stamina by three.

✴ FOCUS CHARM ✴

TRANSFERS YOUR FOCUS TO A TEAMMATE.

Aurors spend most of their time locked in Combat, so they sometimes find themselves sitting on a lot of unused **FOCUS**. Fight the urge to conserve your Focus and use the Auror's **FOCUS CHARM** instead to spread the wealth to teammates when you have ample reserves. Who knows, they may just return the favor by **HEXING** your Foe or healing you up with a **CHARM**.

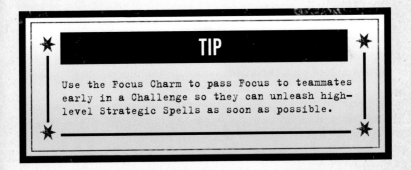

TIP

Use the Focus Charm to pass Focus to teammates early in a Challenge so they can unleash high-level Strategic Spells as soon as possible.

✴ CONFUSION HEX ✴

LOWERS A FOE'S DEFENSE, DODGE, AND DEFENSE BREACH.

The Auror's final Ability significantly **IMPAIRING** several of the Foe's defensive stats. Unleash the **CONFUSION HEX** to breach your Foe's defenses, making them far easier prey for your spells. This ability can be augmented with two additional Lessons, "Confusion Hex Repetitions" and "Confusion Hex Mastery," which, when combined, lowers Enemy Defense by 40 percent, Enemy Dodge by 40 percent, Enemy Defense Breach by 20-40 percent, and Defense Breach de-buff amount by 20 percent.

MAGIZOOLOGIST ABILITIES

Though no strangers to battle, Magizoologists do some of their best work from the sidelines, supporting their comrades in Challenges with **STRATEGIC SPELLS** that can heal and **ENHANCE** teammates. If you have a strong sense of teamwork, or if direct **COMBAT** isn't quite your style, consider taking up the mantle of Magizoology—you'll likely save your team's skin more than once!

✴ STAMINA CHARM ✴

RESTORES AN ALLY'S STAMINA.

The first Strategic Spell every Magizoologist learns is the **STAMINA CHARM**. This magical enchantment instantly restores a significant amount of **STAMINA** to a weary ally, effectively healing their wounds and allowing them to remain in the fray. It's the single strongest **STAMINA** recovery Ability available across all Professions, making the Stamina Charm a major part of every Magizoologist's arsenal. This Ability can be upgraded on two nodes, "Luna's Stamina Charm" and "Stamina Charm Maxima," which will increase the charm's effectiveness by a combined 20-30 percent.

✴ MENDING CHARM ✴

RESTORES AN ALLY'S STAMINA BY A SMALL AMOUNT.

As if one healing Ability weren't enough, Magizoologists soon learn a second healing Ability: the **MENDING CHARM**. Though less effective at restoring **STAMINA**, this charm comes with a shorter cooldown, meaning it can be used more often. Sometimes, a timely bit of healing is all it takes to save a teammate from the brink! This Ability can be augmented on an additional node, "Mending Charm Maxima," which will add two Stamina to the amount you restore.

★ REVIVE CHARM ★

REVIVES A KNOCKED-OUT ALLY AND RESTORES A PORTION OF THEIR STAMINA.

Getting KO'd is no fun, but Magizoologists can spare their teammates this most painful penalty with the **REVIVE CHARM**, a mighty Ability that immediately causes a KO'd ally to recover with a portion of their Stamina restored. Slap on a Stamina Charm afterward for extra healing before sending them back into the fray. You can upgrade this ability with the "Improved Revive Charm" Lesson, which will increase the amount of Stamina restored by 30 percent!

★ BRAVERY CHARM ★

INCREASES AN ALLY'S POWER AGAINST ELITE FOES.

Some Foes are more dangerous than others, and any that feature the title of **ELITE** are sure to be worthy of concern. Fortunately, Magizoologists can learn to empower their allies against these sorts of fearsome Foes. This final Strategic Spell greatly **ENHANCES** a teammate's Expertise in **POWER** when facing **ELITE FOES**, making their spells far more effective against Elites seen in Combat. Augment this Ability with the "Amplified Bravery Charm," which can enhance a teammate's Power against Elites by 90 percent.

PROFESSOR ABILITIES

Blending the Magizoologist's spirit of support with the Auror's penchant for hexes, Professors wield some of the most versatile Strategic Spells of all. They can heal wounded allies, boost their own or their allies DEFENSE, and they even possess the only Ability capable of ENHANCING the entire team at once. They also possess perhaps the most devious hex available to any Profession—one that even Aurors are sure to covet.

✳ DETERIORATION HEX CHARM ✳

LOWERS A FOE'S STAMINA WHENEVER THEY ATTACK OR DEFEND IN COMBAT.

A brutal hex by any stretch, the DETERIORATION HEX punishes the afflicted FOE every time it attacks or defends itself during Combat. This painful IMPAIRMENT has helped many a wizard seize victory in the Arena—slap it on Foes with high defenses to make each round of Combat they endure more painful than the last. Upgrade this Ability with three additional Lessons, "Improve Deterioration Hex," "Deterioration Hex Maxima," and "Deterioration Hex Mastery." When combined, these upgrades impair an enemy's STAMINA by 70 percent!

✳ MENDING CHARM ✳

RESTORES AN ALLY'S STAMINA BY A SMALL AMOUNT.

Borrowing a bit from the Magizoologist's handbook, Professors have learned the value of the Mending Charm, a fast-acting curative Ability that quickly restores a small amount of Stamina to a wounded teammate. This charm lends the Professor some flexibility, letting them play the role of healer when the need arises. Learn the "Mending Charm Maxima" Lesson to increase by two the Stamina you restore to a teammate.

✳ PROTECTION CHARM ✳

INCREASES AN ALLY'S DEFENSE.

This mighty charm boosts the recipient's **DEFENSE**, reducing the damage they suffer from all attacks during Combat. It's a Professor's bread and butter, for once Enhanced by the **PROTECTION CHARM**, teammates won't need quite so much healing all the time. This Ability can be augmented with "Enhanced Protection Charm" and "Perfected Prote ction Charm," which when combined Enhances teammate Defense by 35 percent!

✳ PROFICIENCY POWER CHARM ✳

BOOSTS THE WHOLE TEAM'S PROFICIENCY POWER.

Each Profession has a proficiency advantage over certain types of Foes. For example, Aurors are strongest against **DARK FORCES**, while Magizoologists excel against **BEASTS**. The benefits of this proficiency advantage can be further **ENHANCED** by boosting one's Expertise in **PROFICIENCY POWER**—and that's exactly what the Professor's Proficiency Power Charm does. This final Strategic Spell is so potent that it affects the whole team, causing unlucky Foes with a **DEFICIENCY** drawback to suffer extreme damage in Combat against teammates with superior proficiency! Learn "Perfected Proficiency Charm" and "Advanced Proficiency Charm" to enhance teammate Proficiency Power by up to 44 percent.

★ TEAM COMPOSITION ★

By now, you're likely starting to see how mixing a variety of **PROFESSIONS** can produce teamwide benefits. Aurors might excel at crippling **FOES** in direct Combat, but unless they stockpile Healing Potions, they can't recover **STAMINA** and will find themselves constantly KO'd. Against stiff opposition, a team full of Aurors likely won't have the same chance to succeed as a mixed group of Aurors, Magizoologists, and Professors. Diverse teams have more ways to seize victory—for example, when backed by Magizoologists and Professors, a few Aurors can take on a much stronger horde of Foes, relying on their teammates to support them with healing **ABILITIES** and charms while they focus solely on the **FOE** at hand.

Last, when it comes to seizing victory in tough Wizarding Challenges, you'll want to consider your **PROFESSION BENEFITS** carefully. Look closely at your **LESSON PLAN. LESSONS** that feature red coloring are Profession Benefits. Like **STRATEGIC SPELLS**, Profession Benefits help to define each Profession's Combat capability. For instance, one of the Auror's Profession Benefits makes them more effective against Foes who are below 50 percent Stamina. Aurors who know this Profession Benefit may wish to switch onto Foes with low Stamina during Challenges, quickly finishing them off after other teammates have ground them down.

Take a close look at your Lesson Plan, and try to take Profession Benefits into account when devising your Challenge strategies. Maximizing these Benefits can produce significant advantages that will help your team achieve dominance in even the toughest Wizarding Challenges.

CHAPTER FIVE

CALAMITY CASE FILES

> *"The truth. It is a beautiful and terrible thing, and should therefore be treated with caution."* —*Albus Dumbledore*

If you come across anything, either about the Foundables spell or Grim himself, let me know. I'm afraid if we don't find him — or at least figure out how he did it — we have no chance of undoing what has been done.

Tap to continue

CONSTANCE PICKERING

MYSTERY ITEM
Ministry Memos

REWARDS SUMMARY

The moment you reach **WIZARDING LEVEL 4**, your key contact at the Ministry, **CONSTANCE PICKERING**, reaches out to you. Impressed with your progress thus far, she requests your aid in piecing together the mystery surrounding the **CALAMITY**, deepening your work as a member of the **S.O.S. TASK FORCE**.

From now on, you'll sometimes discover rare **MYSTERY COLLECTIBLES** when you investigate **TRACES** and return **FOUNDABLES**. These Collectibles fit into the **MYSTERIES REGISTRY**, providing vital clues into the Calamity's cause.

A memo from Grim Fawley, addressed to Harry Potter:

"I've never asked anything of you before. But this is Penelope. If you aren't willing to bend the rules for yourself, then do it for her.

Harry, I'm begging you. She's out there. I know it. Please."

NEXT

MINISTRY OF MAGIC

Harry, I'm begging you. She's out there. I know it. Please."

RE: COU[X]DECISION

A memo addressed to Gareth Greengrass from Grim Fawley:

MINISTRY MEMOS
5/5

Grim started as a researcher - that's where he met Penelope. He was quiet, but had a wicked sense of humour.

HARRY POTTER

addressed to Harry Potter:

But when she went missing he changed... I think a piece of him broke.

HARRY POTTER

Harry, I'm begging you. She's out

In this letter he was asking me to break Ministry protocol - to break the law. I wasn't willing to do that.

Tap to continue

HARRY POTTER

Greengrass from Grim Fawley:

You receive detailed notes on each Mystery Collectible you discover, along with a bit of insight provided by one or more of the key characters who are close to the case. Once found, the Mystery Object is stored in the Registry. Unfortunately, the expert testimony cannot be re-accessed. Fortunately, we've taken the liberty of compiling those transcripts here in the **CALAMITY CASE FILE**. Let's have a look at what the investigations have exposed thus far.

The Foundables Spell

By now you've heard the news about the **CALAMITY**, and you've even faced down the consequences of the event, but you have another job too: Help the Ministry find out who caused it and how it can be stopped.

At first the Ministry's leads quickly went cold, but since then several internal **MINISTRY MEMOS** written by the case's central suspect, **GRIM FAWLEY**, have come to light. These documents give insight into how desperate Grim had been to find his wife, **PENELOPE FAWLEY**, one of the London Five. Notions of Grim's desperation are only reinforced when pieces of his very own **JOURNAL** are discovered. It's becoming clear that Grim would do almost anything to get his beloved Penelope back—possibly even something that could change the world.

IMAGE	NAME	COLLECTIBLES
1	*DAILY PROPHET* CLIPPING	1
2	MINISTRY MEMOS	4
3	GRIM FAWLEY'S JOURNAL	5
4	STOLEN BOOKS (INCIDENT REPORT)	1
5	ARCANE TOME	1
6	AMORETTE DENEUVE (LETTER)	1

✷ CHAPTER 1, MYSTERY 1: Evidence ✷

DAILY PROPHET CLIPPING

A clipping from a very old edition of *The Daily Prophet*:

> *The victim, Hamish Steed, was under Ministry protection at the time of Flannery's murderous rampage. After several hours of interrogation, Flannery admitted that he used an ancient spell to track down his greatest desire—which happened to be the location of the late Steed.*

"Someone really used a spell to track down their murder victim?"

CONSTANCE

"That seems impossible . . . And one must not forget that the *Prophet* has a long history of exaggeration."

BRAGNAM

"Funny, we keep records of all their issues, but this one appears to be missing from our archives."

BRAGNAM

MINISTRY MEMO 1: "Re: The Love Room"

A memo from Grim Fawley addressed to Gareth Greengrass, requesting access to the Love Room within the Department of Mysteries. The request was granted.

"Yes, I remember this. Prior to his wife's disappearance, Grim never showed an interest in the Love Room. Poor man, he was completely beside himself when Penelope went missing. I think he just wanted to . . . feel closer to her."

GREENGRASS

"She was one of the missing London Five, yes?"

CONSTANCE

"Yes. Dreadful thing, what happened to her."

GREENGRASS

THE LONDON FIVE

The London Five were a group of five people who went missing mysteriously some years ago. It was never discovered what happened to them and the case was eventually closed. The victims were Penelope Fawley, Riya Patel, Genevieve Bladt, and Timothy Hale, all of whom worked at the Ministry, as well as Kit Gerrard, an investigative reporter for *The Daily Prophet*.

MINISTRY MEMO 2: "Ingredients Invoice"

An order form from Grim Fawley to the Ministry of Magic Remittance Office, requesting a number of potion ingredients, including Baneberry, Jobberknoll Feathers, and Unicorn Hair.

"Hmph. Shows what Mr. Fawley knew. There's no known potion that uses all of these ingredients."

PRICKLE

"Is it possible that Grim was trying to create his own potion? Something completely new?"

CONSTANCE

"Invent his own potion? Grim Fawley?? Hogwash. Potions are a delicate art. A simpleton can't just throw together whatever's in the pantry and expect results. If potion mastery was simple, everyone would do it."

PRICKLE

MINISTRY MEMO 3: "Re: Portkey"

A memo from Grim Fawley, requesting the use of a Portkey. Travel destination: a library in Prague. The request was approved.

"Grim was extremely adamant about traveling to Prague. I never understood why he would need a Portkey. Why not just Apparate?"

GREENGRASS

"What happened to the Portkey?"

CONSTANCE

"We still have it. One never knows when one will need a quick jump to Prague. He never told me what he was looking for in that library. Well, now we know."

GREENGRASS

MINISTRY MEMO 4: "Inter-Library Loan"

Request filed by Grim Fawley for an inter-library loan for an Ancient Tome. Request denied. Appeal filed. Appeal also denied.

"It is unusual for a request to be rejected, but the paperwork here is so very vague . . . I've never heard of this book. Some special research for the Unspeakables, perhaps?"

BRAGNAM

"Not to my knowledge. He shared nothing with me. Grim was very secretive . . ."

GREENGRASS

"Given that he was the obvious source of the Calamity, that is unsurprising."

PRICKLE

GRIM FAWLEY'S JOURNAL 1: "Finding the Spell"

Journal entry written in the small, cramped handwriting of Grim Fawley:

> *There's rumor of a very old, outlawed spell meant to find what one desires most . . . and I may have found it.*
>
> *I don't believe it will bring Penelope back. Not on its own. But maybe I can combine it . . .*

"Combining spells to bring back a loved one. It's genius, in a mad sort of way. Daft, but brilliant."

MYRA

"I can't believe Grim would risk the entire wizarding world just for one person!"

CONSTANCE

"He'd lost his wife, Constance, of course he'd do anything."

MYRA

GRIM FAWLEY'S JOURNAL 2: "The Love Room"

Grim's handwriting is cramped and frantic in a page of his journal:

> *I don't know if it's the Love Room that's causing it, but I feel closer to you here,*
> *Nel. When I'm in here, I KNOW you're alive.*
>
> *It's as if you're just on the other side of a door, and all I have to do is open it.*
> *Is this spell the key?*

"It's possible his mind was
affected by the Love Room."

GREENGRASS

"Is that room
dangerous?"

CONSTANCE

"We cannot know. There's a reason we aren't called 'The Department of
Things We Know Completely' . . ."

"He spent many hours in that room. I got complaints. I can't
help but feel responsible. I gave Grim permission to use the
room in the first place. Maybe I should've kept a closer watch
on him."

GREENGRASS

GRIM FAWLEY'S JOURNAL 3: "Regina Rowle Note"

A note written in swirling handwriting:

> *Now, what would Greengrass think if I told him that his protégé was skulking*
> *about the Love Room after hours? I didn't think you'd be so quick to move on . . .*
> *but . . .*
>
> *Your secret's safe with me. Remember to be careful, Grim. The next time it may*
> *not be me who finds you in there sleeping. ~Regina*

> "Regina Rowle is an Unspeakable. She's also, paradoxically, one of the Ministry's greatest gossips. She's implying that he was using the Love Room to move on from Penelope. But that doesn't seem like Grim."

CONSTANCE

THE LOVE ROOM

The Love Room is located on the ninth floor of the Ministry of Magic, within the Department of Mysteries. It is there that love and its effects are studied, as it is believed by many to be the most powerful force in the world.

GRIM FAWLEY'S JOURNAL 4: "Penelope's Disappearance"

An entry in Grim's journal:

Nel. It's killing me. You always said I was stronger than I knew, but I don't know how to be strong without you.

Harry told me to trust in the Aurors, but they are failing. Miserably. And they are staying so safe . . . Everything is by the book.

If there was something I could do . . . some kind of magic to bring you back, I'd use it in a heartbeat.

> "Grim was desperate—especially after the investigation was called off. He had all kinds of ideas . . . We tried everything to track down Penelope and the other members of the London Five. Followed every lead we could. People don't just disappear like that, there's always some explanation. But this time . . . there was nothing. We're still looking for them—it's unofficial, please don't mention it—but I'll look for them until I find them."

HARRY

GRIM FAWLEY'S JOURNAL 5: "Coded Message"

An entry of letters nonsensically strung together:

53, 14, 6	*xxxiii, 18, 5*	*13, 22, 9*	*xxx, 16, 1*	*48, 12, 2*
7, 12, 6	*36, 9, 2*	*xxv, 12, 8*	*29, 6, 9*	*77, 9, 6!*

Written at the bottom of the page: *Remember, dinner at 8.*

"Oh yes! I've seen these before. It's some sort of Muggle puzzle game. You replace the letters with other letters. And find the words."

MYRA

"Why would Grim be using a Muggle puzzle game?"

CONSTANCE

"Well, it seems that he and Penelope used it with each other—he wrote this note for her.

"Whatever's on it, isn't meant to be easily read, that's for certain."

MYRA

STOLEN BOOKS (Incident Report)

An incident report filed with the Ministry of Magic. A wizarding library in Prague reports that several ancient spell books have gone missing. The librarian believes the thief was a recent visitor.

"I'll eat my wand if this thief wasn't Grim Fawley. I wonder if the library has records of its visitors from the day those books went missing."

CONSTANCE

"My sources in Prague tell me they did an internal investigation and have no leads. And since the Calamity they've become extremely territorial . . . If they do know the thief, they aren't sharing with us."

GREENGRASS

ARCANE TOME

An ancient, dusty tome, hand stitched together and covered in stiff, worn leather. Its contents are written in arcane, faded runes. There are pages ripped from the center of the book.

"My word. This is an extraordinary book. See how it's been bound by hand? These spells are centuries old."

BRAGNAM

"Do you think this might be where Grim Fawley discovered the Foundables spell?"

CONSTANCE

"It's impossible to be sure—there's an entire section of this book that's been ripped out. But, it cannot be ruled out."

MYRA

AMORETTE DENEUVE (Letter)

A handwritten letter from Amorette Deneuve to Grim Fawley:

What makes us yearn for the comfort of others? Why does a broken heart hurt so? Love imbues itself into our very bones, our very souls. I believe that love is the greatest and most dangerous magic in the world.

Along the margin, in cramped writing, reads: —*imbued into our very bones. Use to find her?*

"Amorette Deneuve's the foremost expert on love potions and spells. I've read all of her books—I've even got a signed copy of *First Love, First Loss*! Grim used to tease me for 'putting my faith in such sentimental blather.' Strange that he would contact her like this . . ."

MYRA

THE FOUNDABLES SPELL:
Conclusions

After careful review of the evidence, Grim Fawley is looking awfully guilty.

GRIM CLEARLY MISSED HIS WIFE DEARLY.

o Greengrass noted that Grim wanted access to the Love Room to feel closer to his wife—but is that all there is to it? Regina speculated that Grim was using the Love Room to "move on" from Penelope, though Constance didn't think that was what Grim was after . . .

o Judging from the note and what Harry said, Grim lost faith in the Ministry's ability to find her. Did he take matters into his own hands?

Clearly, Grim was devising a plan to find his wife, but all this evidence looks pretty circumstantial.

o It is fairyly clear that Grim was doing research into a spell that likely caused the Calamity—was that his intention?

He was interested in an old, outlawed spell to find what one desires most—combining the spell with another spell could be dangerous.

o The Ingredients Invoice showed a set of ingredients not known to be combined into a potion. Was he trying to invent something new? Or was he just restocking his own stores with a few things? Either way, Prickle didn't think Grim was any kind of Potions Master . . .

o Interesting that Grim would contact Amorette Deneuve. And that quote—"love is the greatest and most dangerous magic in the world"—feels oddly fitting given the Calamity.

THE CYPHER

o Grim and Penelope used some sort of cypher to communicate. Why would they use a cypher unless they didn't want anyone else knowing what they were up to? What if the Calamity wasn't some sort of spell to find Penelope, but some master plan they formed together . . . one that he was carrying out after her disappearance?

o It's very circumstantial, but it looks like Grim may have been behind the stolen books from Prague. If he was willing to break the law, who knows what he could be capable of?

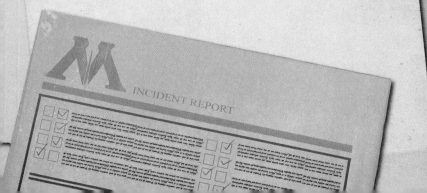

INCIDENT REPORT

CHAPTER 1, MYSTERY 2:

Grim Fawley—Motives

With all evidence pointing to the mysterious Grim Fawley, a closer look into his possible motives seems wise. His desperation to save his lost wife, Penelope, is clear, but most who knew Grim would never think him capable of inflicting the sort of devastation the **CALAMITY** has wrought. A deeper understanding of Grim is needed if the Ministry is to try and pin the Calamity on him.

IMAGE	NAME	COLLECTIBLES
1	MINISTRY MEMOS	5
2	GRIM'S GRIEF (LETTER)	1
3	*DAILY PROPHET* CLIPPING	1
4	PENELOPE'S SCARF	1
5	PENELOPE'S WAND	1
6	LONDON FIVE TRANSCRIPT	1

✳ CHAPTER 1, MYSTERY 2: Evidence ✳

MINISTRY MEMO 1: "Re: Investigation's Closure"

A memo from Grim Fawley, addressed to Harry Potter:

> *I've never asked anything of you before. But this is Penelope. If you aren't willing to bend the rules for yourself, then do it for her.*
>
> *Harry, I'm begging you. She's out there. I know it. Please.*

"Grim started as a researcher—that's where he met Penelope. He was quiet, but had a wicked sense of humor. But when she went missing he changed . . . I think a piece of him broke. In this letter he was asking me to break Ministry protocol—to break the law. I wasn't willing to do that."

HARRY

MINISTRY MEMO 2: "Re: Council Decision"

A memo addressed to Gareth Greengrass from Grim Fawley:

> *You promised me you'd do everything in your power to find Penelope. "No expense spared," you said.*
>
> *But the council's closed the investigation. You're on the bloody council!*
>
> *Please, convince them to re-open the investigation. If not for me, then for Nel.*

"I broke the news to Grim about the investigation's closure about an hour before it was public. He did not take it well. Honestly, it hurt me. I saw Penelope as something of a daughter . . . She was smart, ambitious, stubborn . . . Delightful. Her disappearance nearly destroyed me with grief, but it had been years."

GREENGRASS

MINISTRY MEMOS 3: "Re: Penelope's File"

A Ministry memo addressed to Harry Potter, from Grim Fawley:

> Potter,
> My request to obtain my wife's file has been denied. It is my right to have access to that information.
> Is this how your Department treats its fellow Aurors? Ignore they even existed?
> Barring a grieving husband from the closure he deserves is low, even for you, Potter.

"Grim couldn't leave it alone. He blamed me for the investigation's failure . . . And he had a point . . ."

HARRY

"You did the best you could, Harry."

CONSTANCE

"It wasn't good enough, was it? Regardless, the whole investigation became very political. The files he wanted have been sealed by decree and kept from everyone."

HARRY

MINISTRY MEMOS 4: "Re: Leave of Absence"

A note from Gareth Greengrass, addressed to Grim Fawley:

> Grim,
> I've put in a recommendation that you take time off from work. No one is expecting you to go about your day as if nothing has happened.
> You need time to grieve. We all do. You know Penelope would want you to take care of yourself, for the kids.
> Fondly,
> ~Gareth

"I had to go to the Minister myself to get Grim's leave of absence approved. But it had to be done. His grief was causing problems at work. I was fielding complaints. I had hoped the time off would let him grieve. Help him heal. Apparently it just gave him more time to focus on his obsession."

GREENGRASS

MINISTRY MEMOS 5: "Re: Investigation's Cost"

Filed with the Accounting Department, a memo written by Grim:

> *. . . that budgetary concerns were the reason behind closing the "London Five" investigation. As you can see in the attached, itemized list, the cited reason does not correlate to the actual spending costs. Is this just intentional or accidental stupidity?*
>
> No reply to the memo was sent.

"There were many unseen reasons that the council took into account before we made our decision."

BRAGNAM

"Grim Fawley attempted to appeal the council's ruling eight different times. Eight!"

PRICKLE

"And each time there was a new reason, a new conspiracy . . ."

MYRA

"Not quite the kind of temperament we expect from an Unspeakable, I'm afraid."

PRICKLE

GRIM'S GRIEF (Letter)

A page of Grim's neatly kept journal:

> *Melody has your nose. I never noticed before now, but tonight I came home and realized. And I know you said Addison takes after me, but I swear he has your stubbornness.*
>
> There's a water stain on the page, some letters smudged.
>
> *I'm going to bring you home, Nel. Even if it kills me. Our kids will not grow up like I did.*

"I knew Grim. I worked with him when he first joined the Ministry. Brilliant lad, shy but he had a wit about him. We got on well. When I heard Penelope went missing I was there in case he needed anything . . . But he had changed a bit . . . He was dark. Humorless. Just wanted to talk about the search for his wife and complain about the investigation. We had a falling out. The Grim Fawley I knew couldn't have caused the Calamity, but that Grim? He wasn't someone I knew."

RON

DAILY PROPHET CLIPPING

An issue of *The Daily Prophet*, regarding the Ministry's decision to end its investigation into the London Five:

After failing to come up with any evidence regarding the London Five, the Ministry has shuttered the investigation, leaving families of the missing distraught. Surely an investigation helmed by the famous Harry Potter should have been able to find something?

"It had gone on for months, with no results. A lot of people thought it was time to try different avenues."

PRICKLE

"There was no trace of them. No leads . . . Poor Harry had tried everything— even borrowed some of my creatures."

MATHILDA

"Penelope was a good friend to me . . . But even I had to admit, it was time for the investigation to end."

GREENGRASS

PENELOPE'S SCARF

An old scarf in Slytherin's house colors. The edges are frayed and tattered, and there are several holes in the scarf.

"This was Penelope's scarf. After she went missing, Grim would wear it every day. Even in the summer.

"I always found it a bit sad. He missed her so much . . . But it also started feeling a bit pathetic, if I'm honest."

MATHILDA

PENELOPE'S WAND

The wand is willow, twelve and a half inches long with a dragon heartstring core. There's a large, spindling crack down the middle.

> "That's Penelope Fawley's wand. It was the only thing that was left behind after her disappearance. She was an incredibly skilled Auror. One of the best I've ever seen. When we found out that Penelope was one of the Five that went missing . . . it didn't seem possible that anyone could catch her off guard."

HARRY

LONDON FIVE TRANSCRIPT

Transcript of the Public Hearing given by the Ministry to discuss a motion to terminate the London Five Investigation. Grim Fawley gives a stirring monologue urging the Ministry to keep the investigation open.

GRIM FAWLEY—MOTIVES: Conclusions

A deeper look into Grim Fawley's motives unturned some interesting stones . . .

o The grief-stricken wizard was clearly obsessed with finding his wife, overcome with remorse at her unsolved disappearance. But this doesn't necessarily mean anything—people are generally desperate to find a missing loved one.

o As time passed and the case ran cold, Fawley began butting heads with prominent figures at the Ministry, appealing to re-open the investigation eight times.

o He asked Harry Potter to break the law to help him find Penelope, and also requested access to sealed files, berating Harry when he wouldn't oblige. Grim also hunted down Bragnam and Greengrass, members of the council that decided to close the London Five Investigation.

CONSPIRACY AT THE MINISTRY?

o Grim did accurately point out that the official reason given for closing the investigation ("budgetary concerns") didn't line up with the facts. Could there be a larger cover-up going on? Four of the missing are Ministry officials, after all.

o Feeling utterly lost and alone, Grim may very well have been desperate enough to cast the spell that caused the Calamity, and as an Unspeakable he was entirely capable of researching and executing a spell of that magnitude.

One's past can tell you much about their future. Now that Grim seems to have motive for causing the **CALAMITY**, investigating his background is the next priority. A deeper understanding of the man is needed, for there are still those who would argue on Grim's behalf. Desperate as he was, few believe Fawley truly caused the Calamity to occur.

IMAGE	NAME	COLLECTIBLES
1	FAWLEY URN	1
2	GRIM'S SUITCASE	1
3	WEDDING ANNOUNCEMENT	1
4	NOTE FROM GRIM	1
5	GRIM'S SCHOOL RECORD	1
6	SILVER LOCKET	1

FAWLEY URN

A porcelain urn, covered in a thin layer of dust. The lid is slightly chipped, with an inscription: Lucretia and Marshall Fawley. Loving mother and father.

"Mr. Fawley's parents were killed during the Second Wizarding War, while he was a student at Hogwarts. He was in my Transfiguration class. He was a second year when we were forced to defend the school against Lord Voldemort. He was too young and was sent away. I have always feared he had a very personal lesson in the horrors of war."

MCGONAGALL

GRIM'S SUITCASE

An old, tattered suitcase, the leather on the edges scuffed down to reveal the stretched canvas underneath. The worn nameplate on the top of the case reads "G. M. Fawley." The case is empty inside.

"Grim never talked much about his childhood. I can't imagine what that must have been like, living in orphanages. Seems like a horrible way to grow up, but he never seemed affected by anything . . . Until he lost Penelope."

RON

WEDDING ANNOUNCEMENT

The Daily Prophet, dated June 2006:

Miss Penelope Padgett and Mr. Grim Fawley were wed this past Sunday in West Bromwich. Both Padgett and Fawley work within the Department of Magical Law Enforcement at the Ministry of Magic.

Attached is a picture of Penelope and Grim—Penelope enthusiastically kissing Grim's cheek while he blushes and looks away from the camera.

"Grim was pleasant, but painfully quiet, and Penelope was ... well, ambition's always been a priority amongst Slytherins, hasn't it? And then, suddenly they had two children! I love that photo in the *Prophet*. They look so happy."

CONSTANCE

NOTE FROM GRIM

A handwritten note in Grim's writing, addressed to Penelope:

I've always been the one on the side, looking in on everyone else's adventures. But you're right ... I have a lot to offer. So I'm going to do it ... I'm going to apply to be an Unspeakable. You've got me convinced. I am bloody qualified! It's time to get in the game, right? It's time I had an adventure of my own.

"When he told me he was going to apply to be an Unspeakable I thought it was brilliant. He was perfect for it."

HARRY

"I knew Penelope well and when she mentioned it I thought she was daft ... But then, I thought about it ... Grim Fawley has more magical talent in his little finger than most of us do in our whole bodies. He was a fit."

GREENGRASS

GRIM'S SCHOOL RECORD

A listing of Grim Fawley's achievements as a student at Hogwarts, probably once attached to his CV. It details Fawley's excellent work as a student, receiving five Outstandings and one Exceeds Expectations on his N.E.W.T.s.

"Grim Fawley was an outstanding student. A Hufflepuff through and through. He applied to the Ministry's research wing. If I recall correctly, I wrote him a glowing recommendation."

McGONAGALL

"We were very happy to welcome him into the Department of Magical Law Enforcement. He had qualified to be an Auror if he wanted, but I think he preferred more academic problem solving."

HARRY

SILVER LOCKET

A small silver locket, slightly tarnished from wear; on the inside of the locket is an inscription:

My strength. My heart. My life. G & P

"I remember the two of them were very private about their relationship, at first. It was a bit scandalous, actually. A workplace romance . . . Penelope was older than Grim. Several years, if I recall. But it turns out that they were both more compatible than any of us gave them credit for."

CONSTANCE

GRIM FAWLEY—BACKGROUND:
Conclusions

Grim had a tragic childhood. He was made an orphan by Lord Voldemort's forces and then, months later, he was sent away from Hogwarts on the night of the final battle because he was only a second year student, deemed too young for the fight. Still, Grim seems to have been leading a happy life, thanks in large part to his wife. That all changed when she went missing.

At Hogwarts, Grim was a model student and a Hufflepuff. He entered the Department of Magical Law Enforcement under Harry Potter, where he excelled.

o People seem to have underestimated Grim at every turn—perhaps due to his quiet nature—but he seems to have been a diligent worker with extreme magical talent. Ron noted that the man seemed unfazed by anything until he lost Penelope.

o Could these same people be underestimating Grim when it comes to his possible role in the Calamity?

The Fawleys were clearly deeply in love. In fact, it was Penelope who compelled Grim to strive for the status of Unspeakable.

o Constance mentioned something about Penelope's ambition, though—could this all have been a ruse to gain access to the Ministry's deepest secrets? To the things she and Grim needed to carry out some sort of nefarious plot?

More information is needed about Grim Fawley, for all evidence points to the Calamity as somehow having been his doing. Grim spent most of his time working at the Ministry, so delving into his work record seems likely to produce some clues as to his possible whereabouts. Fawley's likely to have been somehow involved with the Calamity, but more information is needed to track him down.

IMAGE	NAME	COLLECTIBLES
1	UNSPEAKABLES EXPANDING! *(QUIBBLER)*	1
2	TRANSCRIBED TOME	1
3	SKELETON KEY	1
4	UNSPEAKABLES BADGE	1
5	GRIM'S WORK	5
6	REDACTED REPORT	1

UNSPEAKABLES EXPANDING! (*The Quibbler*)

An issue of *The Quibbler*, its headline reading **"THE UNSPEAKABLES EXPAND IN SECRET! WHAT ARE THEY HIDING?"** The issue is dated around the time Grim Fawley was promoted.

"Can I tell you a secret? Sometimes *The Quibbler* gets it right. This was not one of those cases. We had a 143-year-old retire because he kept forgetting everything—literally, everything. Another member wanted to go and write novels. So, we replaced them both—with Grim and Regina Rowle. Simple."

GREENGRASS

TRANSCRIBED TOME

An ancient tome, meticulously cleaned and stored. There are several loose sheaves of paper tucked into the book, scribed in Grim Fawley's small, precise handwriting.

"Fawley was incredibly skilled in rune translation and ancient languages. This particular tome had never been translated. Too difficult, apparently. But Fawley ran through it like it was nothing. He was being wasted with the Aurors . . . I tried to transfer him into my department, but his wife wanted him to be an Unspeakable. And he wanted whatever she wanted . . . In light of recent events, it appears I got very lucky."

BRAGNAM

SKELETON KEY

A mysterious gold key, worn from use.

"That's the key Grim was given upon his promotion to Unspeakable. All Unspeakables are given keys to the Department of Mysteries, and we're the only ones who are allowed into the Department. If this key that you found had somehow gotten into the wrong hands . . . it could have been catastrophic."

GREENGRASS

QUIBBLES WITH *THE QUIBBLER*

The Quibbler, formerly run by Xenophilius Lovegood, is one of the wizarding world's magazines. The publication is known for exploring relatively obscure or unproven topics, but during the Second Wizarding War, it was an invaluable resource of reliable information while *The Daily Prophet* was under the control of Lord Voldemort. Still, not everything in there is considered—er—mainstream news.

UNSPEAKABLES BADGE

A Ministry Identification Card, featuring a photograph of Grim Fawley. The credentials list Fawley as an Unspeakable, with clearance for the Department of Mysteries.

I remember when the rumors started circulating that Grim Fawley was up for promotion to Unspeakable. It seemed like an odd fit—he was so quiet unless you knew him. Being an Unspeakable felt like it was . . . almost above him? I know that sounds harsh, but you had to know him. It was such a jump."

CONSTANCE

GRIM'S WORK 1: "List of New Hires"

An internal Ministry memo, listing new appointments to the Ministry of Magic. Grim Fawley is assigned to the Department of Magical Law Enforcement.

"Grim was assigned to my Department when he first entered the Ministry. I didn't know much about him. He was a research assistant, compiling and fact-checking evidence for the Aurors working in the Department. It's not an easy job; most Aurors don't want to do the paperwork. But Grim was meticulous. He was brilliant."

HARRY

GRIM'S WORK 2: "Grim's Promotion"

A memo written in Gareth Greengrass's elaborate script, announcing the promotion of one Grim Fawley to the role of Unspeakable.

"There were some rumors going around that Gareth Greengrass was showing favoritism to Grim because he was close to Penelope. That's not fair to Grim. He worked very hard. Transferring into that Department is like nothing else. The secrecy, the magical acumen . . . Perhaps Penelope inspired him to pursue the transfer, but the work to get the job? That was all Fawley."

HARRY

GRIM'S WORK 3: "Internal Evaluation"

An evaluation written by Gareth Greengrass and co-signed by Mordecai Berrycloth:

Fawley has shown incredible growth within the Department of Magical Law Enforcement, and has been vital to the apprehension of several Dark wizards. I believe his talents would be an incredible asset to the Department of Mysteries, and I have recommended Fawley to be promoted to Unspeakable.

—Gareth Greengrass

"Mordecai Berrycloth is not just any Auror. His co-signing is probably what pushed Grim's application over the top."

CONSTANCE

"Mordecai wanted to write his own letter, but he settled for a co-signature. That's how much he respected Grim."

HARRY

CONFIDENTIAL

GRIM'S WORK 4: "Year-End Evaluation"

An official Ministry evaluation, dated a year after Grim Fawley joined the Department of Mysteries:

> *Despite personal misgivings regarding Mr. Fawley's commitment to the role, he has surpassed all expectations during his trial period. —Albert Sallow*

"Sallow didn't trust me when I recommended Grim for his promotion. He thought he was too young, too green. Lacked in passion. He didn't see the talent. But eventually Albert saw what I did the year before, and perhaps what we're all seeing now. Grim Fawley is not to be underestimated."

GREENGRASS

GRIM'S WORK 5: "Penelope and Grim"

An Incident report filed with the Department of Magical Law Enforcement, detailing the apprehension of a Dark wizard. The lead Auror on the case was Penelope Padgett, and Grim Fawley was the Head research assistant.

"One year, at a Christmas party, Grim told me that he and Penelope had been going out a year before they told anyone. He was afraid of being transferred out of the department, so they kept it secret. It is quite romantic if you think about it . . . Falling in love as you're solving crimes. The whole thing is like a novel with a bad ending."

CONSTANCE

REDACTED REPORT

Highly redacted official incident report. A thorough reading of the report shows that Grim Fawley appears to have come to the rescue of Ministry Watchwizard Eric Munch in the Department of Mysteries' Brain Room.

MINISTRY RECORD—GRIM FAWLEY:
Conclusions

A thorough check into Grim Fawley's Ministry work record shows him to be an exemplary wizard.

EXPERIENCE IN RUNES AND ANCIENT LANGUAGES

o Grim had a talent for translation, which sheds a bit of light into his secret cypher with Penelope. Could those notes have just been a fun game they were playing? Maybe there isn't anything nefarious about them after all.

o His experience with runes and ancient languages does give him opportunity, however, to explore unregulated and unstable forms of magic—even ones unknown to the Ministry. Bragnam said that the Transcribed Tome we saw had never been translated. Who knows what secrets it held, or if Grim transcribed others like it without reporting their contents back to the Ministry?

He was interested in an old, outlawed spell to find what one desires most—combining the spell with another spell could be dangerous.

UNDERESTIMATING GRIM

o Evidence is growing that many people underestimated Grim, from Constance to his own superiors. People thought he was too young and lacked the passion needed to become an Unspeakable, but he exceeded expectations at every turn.

o Could this be more evidence that Grim really is capable of something like the Calamity? Ron previously noted how much Grim changed after his wife's disappearance . . .

PENELOPE AND GRIM

o Interesting that Penelope and Grim worked on cases together before his transfer to the Department of Mysteries. It would give them a reason to work closely together often.

o No doubt part of their close work was because they were in love and were pulling strings behind the scenes to make it happen, but could they have had another motive for working together as well?

CHAPTER 3, MYSTERY 1:

Penelope Fawley—Background

The investigations into Grim Fawley turned up much intriguing information, but precious little proof. Having failed to find any leads into Fawley's current whereabouts, the case now shifts focus to Grim's wife, the long-lost Penelope Fawley. Born Penelope Padgett, Grim's beloved partner is known to have disappeared mysteriously many years ago—and it is her disappearance that is believed to have sent Fawley over the edge.

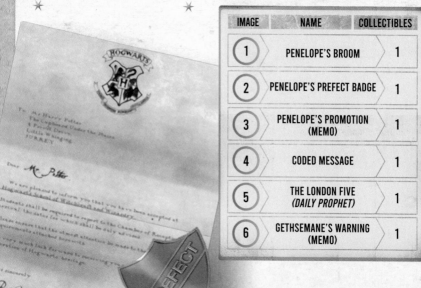

IMAGE	NAME	COLLECTIBLES
1	PENELOPE'S BROOM	1
2	PENELOPE'S PREFECT BADGE	1
3	PENELOPE'S PROMOTION (MEMO)	1
4	CODED MESSAGE	1
5	THE LONDON FIVE (DAILY PROPHET)	1
6	GETHSEMANE'S WARNING (MEMO)	1

PENELOPE'S BROOM

A Comet 290, made by Comet Trading Company. The handle has been worn with age, and "If lost, return to Penelope Padgett" has been magically carved into the wood, near the base of the broom.

"Penelope and I used to talk about Quidditch all the time in the office. She was a huge fan of the Pride of Portree. She told me that her Comet was the last thing she received from her mother before she was sent to Azkaban. It's the only thing she has to remember her by. Penelope favored her broom to travel with during field work instead of Apparating. She said it was because of her motion sickness . . . Now I wonder if she was telling me the whole story . . ."

HARRY

PENELOPE'S PREFECT BADGE

A Prefect Badge in Slytherin's house colors. The metal badge is tarnished and the colors have begun to fade, as if it hasn't been cared for in a while.

"Everyone was worried about Penelope Padgett. It wasn't because she was from Slytherin, mind you. Her parents were open supporters of You-Know-Who . . . Her mum's in Azkaban. There was some reason for a bit of caution."

RON

"Penelope Padgett was one of the finest candidates I've ever seen. No matter who her parents were, she was qualified. And she proved it by becoming a full-fledged Auror within two years of joining our department."

HARRY

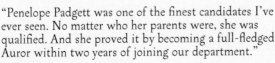

PENELOPE'S PROMOTION (Memo)

An internal Ministry memo written by Harry Potter, announcing Penelope Padgett's promotion to the rank of Auror. The memo details her accomplishments within the Department of Magical Law Enforcement as reason behind the promotion.

"There was no argument—Penelope excelled in her work within the Department. There was an opening and she was the best candidate. But she was never a rule follower. This isn't an uncommon point of view amongst Aurors. Many prefer doing things their own way, and her work was outstanding . . . But when she went missing there wasn't much for me to follow. She was SO secretive . . ."

HARRY

CODED MESSAGE

An encrypted note in Penelope's precise script. It reads:

Darling,
8, 11, 10
53, 14, 6
xxxv, 10, 1
43, 1, 8
73, 18, 9
83, 5, 2
30, 11, 3
3, 16, 7
19, 19, 4
4, 16, 10
5, 6, 3
xiii, 23, 4
xxvii, 14, 4
xxx, 25, 2

xxxv, 16, 7
83, 21, 16
50, 5, 5
88, 4, 4

55, 4, 5
Nel

"This is another of those Muggle puzzles. Unless you know the code, it's useless. She should have just used magic like a normal person. Apparently, she and Fawley liked to communicate in secret. How romantic."

MYRA

THE LONDON FIVE (*The Daily Prophet*)

An issue of *The Daily Prophet*. The headline reads: **"FIVE GO MISSING IN LONDON—INVESTIGATION UNDERWAY."** The *Prophet* lists the missing: Riya Patel, Timothy Hale, Kit Gerrard, Genevieve Bladt, and Penelope Fawley.

"The London Five. The Ministry never had an event quite like this before—five disappearances all within a few hours, with no evidence, and no witnesses. Someone was capable of making Aurors disappear without a trace . . . The story took hold across the entire wizarding world."

MATHILDA

GETHSEMANE'S WARNING (Memo)

A Ministry memo addressed to Harry Potter,
from Gethsemane Prickle:

Be careful with that Padgett woman, Potter. Her parents were followers of You-Know-Who, and you know the apple rarely falls far from the tree. She's trouble, mark my words.

"I warned them about her then, and now I have been proven correct. A dirigible plum doesn't just float away from the bush."

PRICKLE

"Penelope has been missing for years."

CONSTANCE

"Exactly. Totally gone. Even Potter can't find her. And now, coincidently, her husband has caused the Calamity. If you think the Calamity isn't tied to her disappearance, you are naive."

PRICKLE

PENELOPE FAWLEY—BACKGROUND:
Conclusions

Probing into the past of one Penelope Padgett Fawley turns out to be quite the fascinating journey.

DIFFERENT WORLDS

o Curiously, the fact that Grim and Penelope's parents were on opposing sides of the Second Wizarding War didn't seem to affect their love. Similarly, Harry wasn't bothered having her on his staff, despite her family history.

o Could this mean that Grim shared some sort of Dark aim? Or is it just his Hufflepuff nature of tolerance and equality, seeing the best in his wife no matter what was in her family's past?

o This wasn't true of everyone in the Ministry, however. Plenty of people—including Ron—mistrusted Penelope because of her parents' deeds.

o When the Calamity occurred and Grim was wanted for questioning, many others, including Prickle, turned a suspicious eye on Penelope and her past. But could she have really had a hand in the Calamity when she's been missing for years?

PENELOPE'S NATURE

o Penelope was naturally quite secretive. According to Harry, this made it much harder to find any leads regarding her disappearance. Strangely, Grim seems less interested in why she disappeared than in how to get her back. Could he have some knowledge that we don't?

o Harry noted that Penelope was never much of a rule follower, though this certainly doesn't mean she was guilty of any crimes.

o Penelope was an extremely gifted Auror who was promoted by Harry Potter himself during her time at the Ministry's Department of Magical Law Enforcement.

Darling,
48, 17, 6
xxxiv, 7, 9
5, 2, 7
xxxiii, 9, 6
85, 8, 6
77, 18, 9
24, 2, 5
xvi, 12, 4
37, 4, 2
53, 14, 6

79, 4, 4
67, 11, 9
19, 12, 6
42, 15, 1
82, 15, 7

51, 18, 13
55, 1, 5
xv, 22, 2

xvi, 14, 10
Nel

Whoever caused the Calamity, the whole event seems somehow tied to Grim Fawley, his wife, Penelope, and the tragic event from the past in which she and four others disappeared. The curious case of the Calamity remains unsolved for the moment, but rest assured that the Ministry is on the job. Stay vigilant, wizard, and be sure to report any future findings to the Ministry straightaway!

CHAPTER SIX

LOST AND FOUNDABLES

> *"Things we lose have a way of coming back to us in the end, if not always in the way we expect."* —Luna Lovegood

If you've made it this far, you're no doubt looking to complete your **REGISTRY**. The pages that follow showcase completed **EXPLORATION**, **CHALLENGE**, and **ADVERSARY REGISTRY PAGES**.

As you may well know, the Registry features four sections: **EXPLORATIONS**, **MYSTERIES**, **CHALLENGES**, and **EVENTS**.

⭒ **EXPLORATIONS:** Foundables that can be returned by investigating **TRACES** you discover on the Map (p. 140).

⭒ **MYSTERIES:** Foundables that provide clues to the mystery surrounding the **CALAMITY** (p. 106).

⭒ **CHALLENGES:** Foundables that can be returned when you succeed at **WIZARDING CHALLENGES** (p. 154).

⭒ **ADVERSARIES:** Foundables that can be returned when fighting special **ADVERSARIES** (p. 168).

Each Registry Page is blank at first, showing only silhouettes of the Foundables that belong to that Page's associated **FAMILY OF MAGIC**. By returning Foundables that belong to each **REGISTRY FAMILY**, you'll steadily fill in their **IMAGES** on the Registry Pages, reaping some excellent rewards in the process.

Gobstone Set
LOW

SEEN: 1   **FRAGMENTS : 1**

A messy children's game similar to marbles where, when a player loses a point, a gobstone will spray putrid liquid on the player. Despite its reputation as a children's game, the Gobstones World Championship is taken very seriously by afficionados.

RETURNED: FRIDAY, 03 MAY 2019

FOUND AT: SAN FRANCISCO, UNITED STATES

RETURNED TO: SLYTHERIN COMMON ROOM

X

Wizards Unite rewards you each time you return a Foundable and any time you complete a Wizarding Challenge or progress through a special **EVENT**. Many times, the rewards include **FRAGMENTS** of a Foundable's Image for your Registry. Foundables that feature lower **THREAT LEVELS** require fewer Fragments for their Images, while those of a higher Threat Level require more. The number of Fragments needed to complete each Image is shown near the base of the Image's silhouette.

✷ EXPLORATION REGISTRY ✷

The best way to fill your **EXPLORATION REGISTRY** is to get out there and pound the pavement in search of **TRACES**. Each Trace that pops up on the **MAP** features a **FAMILY ICON** that relates to the Exploration Registry's **PAGES**—use **LANDMARKS** to seek out Traces for the precise Pages you need to fill.

✷ ✷ ✷ **FAMILY ICONS** ✷ ✷ ✷

CARE OF MAGICAL CREATURES	MINISTRY OF MAGIC	MYSTERIOUS ARTIFACTS
DARK ARTS	MAGIZOOLOGY	WONDERS OF THE WIZARDING WORLD
HOGWARTS SCHOOL	MAGICAL GAMES AND SPORTS	ODDITIES*
LEGENDS OF HOGWARTS		

* **ODDITIES** are the only Registry Pages not shown here. See p. 34 for details instead.

HAGRID'S HUT

IMAGE	NAME
1	ABRAXAN WINGED HORSE
2	HAGRID'S HUT
3	RUBEUS HAGRID
4	BUCKBEAK
5	BABY NORWEGIAN RIDGEBACK

PUMPKIN PATCH

IMAGE	NAME
1	MONSTER BOOK OF MONSTERS
2	BABY HIPPOGRIFF
3	FLOBBERWORM
4	KNEAZLE
5	ACROMANTULA EGGS

FORBIDDEN FOREST

IMAGE	NAME
1	HIPPOGRIFF (BROWN)
2	CENTAUR—FIRENZE
3	BABY UNICORN
4	BLAST-ENDED SKREWT
5	DRAGON EGG
6	PUFFSKEIN

BORGIN & BURKES

IMAGE	NAME
1	WANTED POSTER: AZKABAN ESCAPEE
2	*MAGICK MOSTE EVILE* BOOK
3	VANISHING CABINET
4	FLESH-EATING SLUGS
5	HAND OF GLORY

KNOCKTURN ALLEY

IMAGE	NAME
1	SWOOPING EVIL
2	KNOCKTURN ALLEY SIGN
3	WIZARD PORTRAIT— BELLATRIX LESTRANGE
4	HAG
5	THESTRAL
6	MINISTRY EXECUTIONER

FALLEN MINISTRY ATRIUM

IMAGE	NAME
1	PERCIVAL GRAVES
2	TOM RIDDLE
3	PORTRAIT OF VOLDEMORT
4	TOM RIDDLE SR'S GRAVESTONE
5	MAGIC IS MIGHT STATUE

DADA CLASSROOM

9¾

IMAGE	NAME
1	GRYFFINDOR STUDENT
2	RAVENCLAW STUDENT
3	HUFFLEPUFF STUDENT
4	BOGGART CABINET
5	SLYTHERIN STUDENT

9¾ MOVING STAIRCASES

IMAGE	NAME
1	FILIUS FLITWICK
2	HEADMISTRESS MCGONAGALL
3	PEEVES
4	POMONA SPROUT
5	HOGWARTS HOUSE CUP
6	MOANING MYRTLE

9¾ GREAT HALL

IMAGE	NAME
1	PHOENIX—FAWKES
2	WIZARD PORTRAIT—HEADMASTER DUMBLEDORE
3	HOUSE HOURGLASS SET
4	OWL LECTERN
5	SORTING HAT

ROOM OF REQUIREMENT—
DUMBLEDORE'S ARMY

IMAGE	NAME
1	FILCH AND MRS. NORRIS
2	YOUNG NEVILLE LONGBOTTOM IN STREET CLOTHES
3	YOUNG GINNY WEASLEY IN STREET CLOTHES
4	YOUNG LUNA LOVEGOOD IN STREET CLOTHES
5	D.A. PRACTICE DUMMY
6	WEASLEY FIREWORKS

POTIONS
CLASSROOM

IMAGE	NAME
1	HEDWIG
2	YOUNG HARRY POTTER IN STREET CLOTHES
3	SEVERUS SNAPE
4	SIRIUS BLACK
5	HALF-BLOOD PRINCE'S COPY OF *ADVANCED POTION-MAKING*

CHESS CHAMBER

IMAGE	NAME
1	FLYING KEY
2	WIZARD CHESS QUEEN
3	ALBUS DUMBLEDORE IN GOBLET OF FIRE OUTFIT
4	YOUNG HERMIONE GRANGER IN STREET CLOTHES
5	YOUNG RON WEASLEY IN STREET CLOTHES

MINISTRY ATRIUM

IMAGE	NAME
1	FLOCK OF INTER-DEPARTMENTAL MEMOS
2	MINISTRY OFFICIAL
3	*DAILY PROPHET* STAND
4	MINISTRY ADMINISTRATOR
5	PROPHECY ORB

MINISTRY ATRIUM II

IMAGE	NAME
1	FOUNTAIN OF MAGICAL BRETHREN
2	THE VEIL
3	BOGROD
4	TANK OF BRAINS
5	NEWT SCAMANDER

COURTROOM TEN

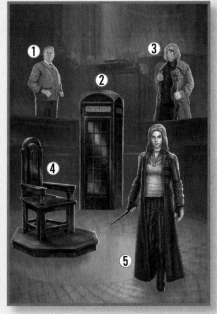

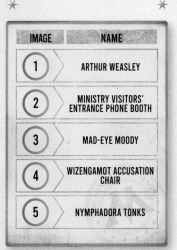

IMAGE	NAME
1	ARTHUR WEASLEY
2	MINISTRY VISITORS' ENTRANCE PHONE BOOTH
3	MAD-EYE MOODY
4	WIZENGAMOT ACCUSATION CHAIR
5	NYMPHADORA TONKS

NEWT'S CASE

IMAGE	NAME
1	BILLYWIG
2	YOUNG GRAPHORN
3	NIFFLER
4	BABY NIFFLER
5	MOONCALF

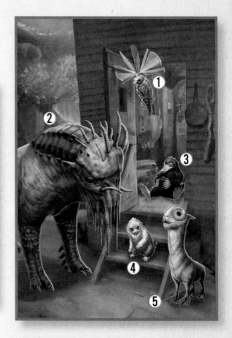

CENTRAL PARK

IMAGE	NAME
1	MOUNTAIN TROLL
2	ERUMPENT
3	DEMIGUISE
4	BRANCH OF BOWTRUCKLES
5	PICKETT
6	MURTLAP

NEW YORK CITY STREET

IMAGE	NAME
1	THUNDERBIRD
2	OCCAMY
3	YOUNG NEWT SCAMANDER *(FANTASTIC BEASTS)*
4	UNICORN
5	OCCAMY EGGS

WORLD CUP GROUNDS

IMAGE	NAME
1	GOBSTONE SET
2	QUAFFLE
3	MAGICAL MEGAPHONE
4	QUIDDITCH WORLD CUP
5	CHUDLEY CANNONS PLAYER

HOGWARTS QUIDDITCH PITCH

IMAGE	NAME
1	QUIDDITCH PITCH STANDS (TOWERS)
2	BLUDGER
3	GOLDEN SNITCH
4	QUIDDITCH KEEPER RON
5	BEATER'S BAT
6	EXPLODING SNAP CARDS

TRIWIZARD MAZE

IMAGE	NAME
1	NIMBUS 2000
2	YOUNG HARRY POTTER GRYFFINDOR QUIDDITCH CAPTAIN
3	GOBLET OF FIRE
4	TRIWIZARD CUP
5	*QUIDDITCH THROUGH THE AGES* BOOK

ROOM OF REQUIREMENT

IMAGE	NAME
1	QUILL OF ACCEPTANCE AND BOOK OF ADMITTANCE
2	WEASLEY CLOCK
3	REMEMBRALL
4	HAGRID'S UMBRELLA
5	DECOY DETONATORS

DUMBLEDORE'S OFFICE

IMAGE	NAME
1	MIRROR OF ERISED
2	SWORD OF GRYFFINDOR
3	PENSIEVE
4	SORCERER'S STONE
5	DUMBLEDORE'S MEMORY CABINET

ROOM OF REQUIREMENT—
HIDDEN THINGS

IMAGE	NAME
1	OPAL NECKLACE
2	MARAUDER'S MAP
3	HERMIONE'S TIME-TURNER
4	OMNIOCULARS
5	MAD-EYE MOODY'S EYE
6	SIRIUS'S FLYING MOTORBIKE

ROOM OF REQUIREMENT—
HIDDEN THINGS

IMAGE	NAME
1	SELF-PLAYING HARP
2	DIRIGIBLE PLUM
3	CRYSTAL BALL
4	MUSIC BOX
5	*QUIBBLER*

HOGWARTS GATE

IMAGE	NAME
1	HOWLER
2	WHOMPING WILLOW
3	FLYING CAR
4	THE KNIGHT BUS
5	GRAWP THE GIANT
6	WANTED POSTER: SIRIUS BLACK

KING'S CROSS STATION

IMAGE	NAME
1	PLATFORM NINE AND THREE-QUARTERS SIGN
2	THE HOGWARTS EXPRESS ENGINE
3	FOE-GLASS WITH SUBTLE CAT SILHOUETTE
4	BABY MANDRAKE
5	GIANT'S HELM

★ CHALLENGE REGISTRY ★

When you're ready to ramp up the action, plot a course to the nearest **FORTRESS** and test your mettle in the thrilling **WIZARDING CHALLENGES** held there. Up to five wizards can unite to experience the rush of **COMBAT** against a Fortress's many **CHAMBERS** of **FOES**. Securing victory in each chamber unlocks the next one ahead, and also earns you some exceptional prizes, including **IMAGE FRAGMENTS** for your **CHALLENGE REGISTRY**, and precious **SPELL BOOKS** to help you through your **LESSON PLAN** (p. 56)!

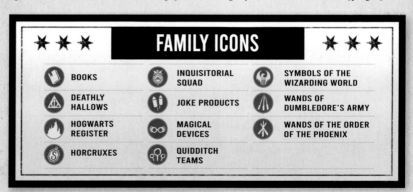

★★★ FAMILY ICONS ★★★

- BOOKS
- DEATHLY HALLOWS
- HOGWARTS REGISTER
- HORCRUXES
- INQUISITORIAL SQUAD
- JOKE PRODUCTS
- MAGICAL DEVICES
- QUIDDITCH TEAMS
- SYMBOLS OF THE WIZARDING WORLD
- WANDS OF DUMBLEDORE'S ARMY
- WANDS OF THE ORDER OF THE PHOENIX

📖 BOOKS I

IMAGE	NAME
1	*HOGWARTS: A HISTORY*
2	*MAGICAL WATERPLANTS OF THE MEDITERRANEAN*
3	*A BEGINNER'S GUIDE TO TRANSFIGURATION*
4	*ADVANCED RUNE TRANSLATION*
5	*UNFOGGING THE FUTURE*

BOOKS II

IMAGE	NAME
1	THE ESSENTIAL DEFENSE AGAINST THE DARK ARTS
2	A HISTORY OF MAGIC
3	MOSTE POTENTE POTIONS
4	THE STANDARD BOOK OF SPELLS
5	A NEW THEORY OF NUMEROLOGY

BOOKS III

IMAGE	NAME
1	EASY SPELLS TO FOOL MUGGLES
2	THE ADVENTURES OF MARTIN MIGGS, THE MAD MUGGLE
3	THE TALES OF BEEDLE THE BARD
4	THE LIFE AND LIES OF ALBUS DUMBLEDORE
5	POKERY AND HOCUS POCUS

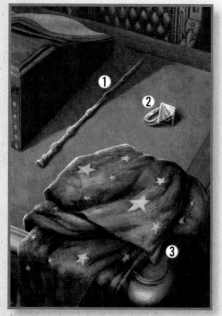

DEATHLY HALLOWS

IMAGE	NAME
1	ELDER WAND
2	RESURRECTION STONE
3	INVISIBILITY CLOAK

HOGWARTS REGISTER I

IMAGE	NAME
1	RUBEUS HAGRID
2	ALBUS DUMBLEDORE IN SORCERER'S STONE OUTFIT
3	SEVERUS SNAPE
4	MINERVA McGONAGALL— YULE BALL

HOGWARTS REGISTER II

IMAGE	NAME
1	YOUNG HARRY POTTER IN STREET CLOTHES
2	YOUNG RON WEASLEY IN STREET CLOTHES
3	YOUNG HERMIONE GRANGER IN STREET CLOTHES

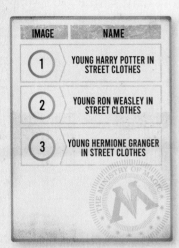

HOGWARTS REGISTER III

IMAGE	NAME
1	NEARLY HEADLESS NICK
2	BLOODY BARON
3	GRAY LADY
4	FAT FRIAR

HOGWARTS REGISTER IV

IMAGE	NAME
1	YOUNG LUNA LOVEGOOD IN RAVENCLAW ROBES WITH SPECTRESPECS
2	YOUNG NEVILLE LONGBOTTOM IN GRYFFINDOR ROBES WITH TREVOR THE TOAD
3	YOUNG GINNY WEASLEY IN GRYFFINDOR ROBES

HORCRUXES I

IMAGE	NAME
1	HUFFLEPUFF'S CUP
2	TOM RIDDLE'S DIARY
3	RAVENCLAW'S DIADEM
4	SLYTHERIN'S LOCKET

HORCRUXES II

IMAGE	NAME
1	YOUNG HARRY IN *H* SWEATER
2	NAGINI
3	MARVOLO GAUNT'S RING

INQUISITORIAL SQUAD I

IMAGE	NAME
1	MILLICENT BULSTRODE—INQUISITORIAL SQUAD
2	DOLORES UMBRIDGE IN HIGH INQUISITOR OUTFIT
3	PANSY PARKINSON—INQUISITORIAL SQUAD
4	VERITASERUM

IMAGE	NAME
1	INQUISITORIAL SQUAD BADGE
2	GREGORY GOYLE— INQUISITORIAL SQUAD
3	DRACO MALFOY— INQUISITORIAL SQUAD
4	VINCENT CRABBE— INQUISITORIAL SQUAD

JOKE PRODUCTS I

IMAGE	NAME
1	EXTENDABLE EARS
2	EXPLODING WHIZZ POPPER
3	NOSE-BITING TEACUP
4	DUNGBOMB

JOKE PRODUCTS II

IMAGE	NAME
1	U-NO-POO
2	FANGED FRISBEE
3	SCREAMING YO-YO
4	TRICK WAND

JOKE PRODUCTS III

IMAGE	NAME
1	CANARY CREAME
2	SKIVING SNACKBOX
3	PORTABLE SWAMP

MAGICAL DEVICES I

IMAGE	NAME
1	MINISTRY TIME-TURNER
2	PROBITY PROBE
3	RITA SKEETER'S QUICK-QUOTES QUILL
4	MAD-EYE MOODY'S SNEAKOSCOPE

MAGICAL DEVICES II

IMAGE	NAME
1	SECRECY SENSOR
2	SPECTRESPECS
3	DELUMINATOR
4	HARRY/SIRIUS TWO-WAY MIRROR

QUIDDITCH TEAMS I

IMAGE	NAME
1	MONTROSE MAGPIES
2	PUDDLEMERE UNITED
3	TARAPOTO TREE-SKIMMERS
4	SWEETWATER ALL-STARS
5	BALLYCASTLE BATS

QUIDDITCH TEAMS II

IMAGE	NAME
1	MOOSE JAW METEORITES
2	WOLLONGONG WARRIORS
3	CHUDLEY CANNONS
4	QUIBERON QUAFFLEPUNCHERS
5	GRODZISK GOBLINS

IMAGE	NAME
1	PRIDE OF PORTREE
2	HOLYHEAD HARPIES
3	TOYOHASHI TENGU
4	TUTSHILL TORNADOS
5	GIMBI GIANT-SLAYERS

SYMBOLS OF THE WIZARDING WORLD I

IMAGE	NAME
1	DARK MARK
2	MINISTRY
3	MACUSA
4	DEATHLY HALLOWS

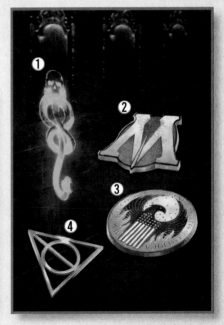

SYMBOLS OF THE WIZARDING WORLD II

IMAGE	NAME
1	GRYFFINDOR
2	SLYTHERIN
3	HOGWARTS
4	HUFFLEPUFF
5	RAVENCLAW

SYMBOLS OF THE WIZARDING WORLD III

IMAGE	NAME
1	DEPARTMENT OF MAGICAL LAW ENFORCEMENT
2	DEPARTMENT FOR THE REGULATION AND CONTROL OF MAGICAL CREATURES
3	DEPARTMENT OF MAGICAL ACCIDENTS AND CATASTROPHES
4	DEPARTMENT OF INTERNATIONAL MAGICAL COOPERATION
5	DEPARTMENT OF MAGICAL TRANSPORTATION

WANDS OF DUMBLEDORE'S ARMY I

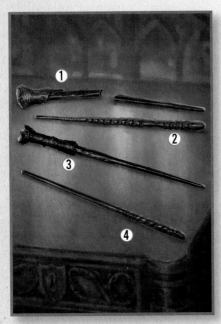

IMAGE	NAME
1	RON WEASLEY'S WAND (BROKEN)
2	CHO CHANG'S WAND
3	HARRY POTTER'S WAND
4	GINNY WEASLEY'S WAND

WANDS OF DUMBLEDORE'S ARMY II

IMAGE	NAME
1	FRED WEASLEY'S WAND
2	GEORGE WEASLEY'S WAND
3	LUNA LOVEGOOD'S WAND
4	HERMIONE GRANGER'S WAND
5	NEVILLE LONGBOTTOM'S WAND

WANDS OF THE ORDER OF THE PHOENIX I

IMAGE	NAME
1	REMUS LUPIN'S WAND
2	SEVERUS SNAPE'S WAND
3	MAD-EYE MOODY'S WAND
4	MINERVA McGONAGALL'S WAND

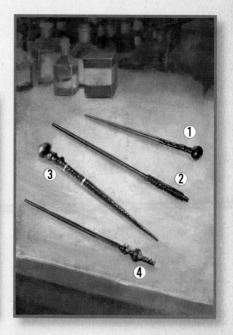

WANDS OF THE ORDER OF THE PHOENIX II

IMAGE	NAME
1	MOLLY WEASLEY'S WAND
2	BILL WEASLEY'S WAND
3	ARTHUR WEASLEY'S WAND
4	FLEUR DELACOUR'S WAND

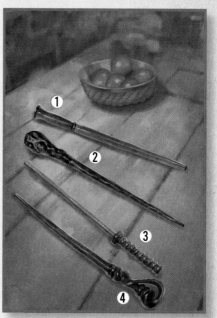

WANDS OF THE ORDER OF THE PHOENIX III

IMAGE	NAME
1	KINGSLEY SHACKLEBOLT'S WAND
2	MUNDUNGUS FLETCHER'S WAND
3	SIRIUS BLACK'S WAND
4	NYMPHADORA TONKS'S WAND

RICERCATO

DAL

⁎ ADVERSARIES REGISTRY ⁎

Tucked away at the far left end of the **CHALLENGES REGISTRY**, four special sections combine to form the **ADVERSARY REGISTRY**. These are included here because we can only speculate about how and when the **FOES** will appear.

Voldemort's Army

Death Eaters

Hogwarts Villains

Ancient Dragons

⁎ ACERCARSE CON EXTREMA CAUTELA ⁎

LORD VOLDEMORT

HITTA FYNDIGHETERNA! KONTROLLERA KATASTROFEN!

PELIGRO

PROCURARSE CON MUCHO CUIDADO

UNISSEZ

MINISTRY OF MAGIC
DEPARTMENT OF SECRECY

BELLATRIX LESTRANGE

FIGHT

協力して大災厄に立ち向かえ

LUCIUS MALFOY

БУДЬТЕ НАЧЕКУ

MINISTRY OF MAGIC

 NARCISSA MALFOY

RICERCATO

DAL MINISTERO DELLA MAGIA

★ GÅ YDERST FORSI

끊임없이 경계하라

 FENRIR GREYBACK

UNITE

...MITY

...MAGIE ★

TO FIGHT

IAKTTA STÖRSTA FÖRSIKTIGHET

GEVAR

맞서라

Constance Pickering
CONSTANCE PICKERING

BARTY
CROUCH JR.

GEZOCHT

✳ DOOR HET MINISTERIE VAN TOVERKUNST ✳

PETER
PETTIGREW

維持魔法的隱秘性，讓麻瓜渾

ZACHOWAJ CZUJNOŚĆ

DAS DESASTER VEREINT BEKÄMPFEN

...ILÂNCIA CONSTANTE

Constance Pickering
CONSTANCE PICKERING

**DOLORES
UMBRIDGE**

**DRACO
MALFOY**

HOLD MAGIEN HEMMELIG.SKJUL ALT FRA GOMPENE

CONTENEZ

LA CALAMIT...

MINISTRY OF MAGIC
DEPARTMENT OF SECRECY

**SLYTHERIN'S
BASILISK**

RETURNER FINDERIET

ANCIENT HUNGARIAN HORNTAIL

ELORDEN. DEVCL

GILDEROY LOCKHART

İENLİKE

BÜYÜ BAKANLIĞI BİLDİRİSİ

ARAGOG

* MIT EXTREMER VORSICHT VORGEHEN *

ANCIENT UKRAINIAN IRONBELLY

POWSTRZYMAJ KATASTROFĘPOWSTRZYMAJ

ANCIENT NORWEGIAN RIDGEBACK

THE
WIZARDING
WORLD
— IS AT RISK OF —
EXPOSURE
WE NEED YOUR HELP

WIZARDS
UNITE